# I, Monster: A New Model for Understanding Sin, Death, and Human Nature

Step into the Gospel as you've rarely been invited to see it—not first as a private solution to personal guilt, but as a public story of creation, invasion, and rescue. *I, Monster* reframes the Gospel as a cosmic drama in which God's good cosmos has not merely been "broken" by human mistakes but occupied by hostile powers that deform humanity and corrupt creation itself.

At the center of this story stand two enemies, twin chaos-forces the Bible treats with striking seriousness: Sin and Death. In Scripture—and in the wider ancient Near Eastern imagination—these are not only abstract ideas. They are portrayed as living, active forces: invaders that seize territory, enslave human beings, and bend the world toward decay. *I, Monster* traces how these powers infiltrate the human self, turning it into contested space—a battleground where divine purpose clashes with primal chaos, and where humans become capable of turning against God, against one another, and against themselves.

But this is not a story of despair. It is the Gospel's announcement of hope. The death and resurrection of Christ are not merely symbolic comforts or legal transactions. They are a direct confrontation with enemy rule. Jesus challenges the reign of Sin and Death, breaks their claim on humanity, curbs their power in the present, and guarantees their ultimate defeat. Moving through Genesis, Israel's Scriptures, the Gospels, Paul's letters, and other key biblical texts, this book shows how Christ's work is aimed not at shaming you for your mistakes but at liberating and restoring you—because humans are not the true enemies of God. The real enemies are the forces that enslave and destroy.

Along the way, *I, Monster* explores humanity's hybrid nature—formed from earth and filled with God's divine breath—and argues that the human self can appear "monstrous" precisely because it is the place where these invading powers do their work. Yet it is also the place where God's Spirit dwells, offering hope, peace, renewal, presence, and glorious transformation. Drawing on biblical theology, ancient context, and modern monster theory, this book offers a fresh vision of the Gospel itself: what has gone wrong with the world, what Christ has done to set it right, and what it means to be human in light of God's victory.

Whether you're a theologian, a pastor, or a thoughtful reader who senses that the Gospel has been taught too narrowly, *I, Monster* invites you to see Scripture's story whole again—and to rediscover the hope at its center.

# I, Monster: A New Model for Understanding Sin, Death, and Human Nature

Why the Gospel Story Is Bigger than Sin, Guilt, and Shame
And How Christ Defeats the Monsters Within

Dr Tyson Putthoff

# Hekhal Publishing Co.

‖‖‖‖‖‖‖‖‖‖‖‖‖‖‖
I0453798

**Hekhal Publishing Co.** is dedicated to producing works that bridge the gap between academic scholarship and practical application, offering fresh, cutting-edge perspectives on biblical studies, theology, and the ancient world. Our mission is to make complex ideas accessible, engaging, and transformative.

For more information, visit: https://www.hekhal.co

© **Hekhal Publishing Co. 2026**

Hekhal Publishing Co. | North America

First published 2026

AUTHOR: Tyson Putthoff
I, Monster: A New Model for Understanding Sin, Death, and Human Nature | Includes bibliographical references and indexes

LCCN: 2025951431
ISBN (hardcover): 979-8-9985268-8-6
ISBN (paperback): 979-8-9985268-6-2
ISBN (ebook): 979-8-9985268-7-9

HEKHAL PUB. CO. CID: 46714-00931

SUBJECTS: Bible—Anthropology; Monsters in the Bible; Hebrew Bible/Old Testament; Ancient Near East—Religion; Biblical Theology; Theological Anthropology—Christianity

Set in Cambria and Calibri.

**Hekhal Publishing Co.** is not responsible for the persistence or accuracy of URLs for external or third-party websites referenced in this publication, nor does it guarantee that any linked content will remain available or appropriate.

iii

The dual substance of Christ—the yearning, so human, so superhuman, of man to attain God or, more exactly, to return to God and identify himself with him—has always been a deep, inscrutable mystery to me. This nostalgia for God, at once so mysterious and so real, has opened in me large wounds and also large flowing springs.

My principal anguish—and the source of all my joys and sorrows from my youth onward—has been the incessant, merciless battle between the spirit and the flesh.

*Within me are the dark immemorial forces of the Evil One, human and pre-human; within me too are the luminous forces, human and pre-human, of God—and my soul is the arena where these two armies have clashed and met.*

Nikos Kazantzakis, *The Last Temptation of Christ*
Originally published in 1955
Translated in 1960
Italics my own

# NOTE FROM THE AUTHOR

This book didn't begin as a book. It began as two parallel paths in my life—one academic, one deeply personal—that slowly converged until I couldn't tell them apart. Only then did I realize I wasn't writing an argument; I was writing out of my own life.

The academic journey stretches back to 2017, when I published *Ontological Aspects of Early Jewish Anthropology* with Brill. That project opened the door for me into ancient ideas of how gods and spiritual beings could inhabit human bodies. At the time, I was simply trying to understand how embodiment, indwelling, and transformation worked in the ancient imagination. I didn't yet see where that path would lead.

Then came 2020, when *Gods and Humans in the Ancient Near East* was published by Cambridge University Press. That book was not about monsters at all. It was about how ancient people imagined humanity as divine-adjacent beings, porous to outside forces, capable of hosting divine presence—good or bad. But it was during that project, almost in passing, that I stumbled upon something that shook me: divinity in the ancient world was not automatically benevolent. To be "filled with a god" could be ecstatic, terrifying, destabilizing, or even destructive. And in chapter 3, footnote 83, to be exact, while discussing humanity's creation from the remains of Tiamat's monstrous body, I found myself seeing that, in the ancient imagination, humanity bears a trace of that monstrous origin and that I'd explore it in a future volume.

I didn't know it then, as that led me into a more academic engagement with the subject of monstrosity in the ancient world. But it turns out that that sentence would end up being the seed of this book.

But my interest in the monstrous did not begin there. Long before I was writing academic monographs, I was fascinated by monsters in a far more instinctive way. Growing up in the 1980s, I spent many nights at my best friend's house watching horror movies we absolutely shouldn't have been watching at that age—the slashers, the creature features, possessions, anything that blurred fear and fascination. In sixth grade, I was reading Stephen King during silent reading time and writing horror stories with my friend during writing time—crude, over-the-top, but thrilling. At that same time, my fascination with Venom comics also began to take shape. That early interest in the monstrous never fully left. I don't watch many horror films now, but something in me has always been drawn to the edges of things—the boundary where terror, meaning, embodiment, and mystery collide.

At the same time, I grew up—and spent much of my life—within a conservative Christian culture whose Gospel centered around shame. It was during a period in American Evangelicalism when the predominant voices in culture, parenting, and morality greatly shaped the theological messaging that many from my generation still carry. This was simply the theological water we all swam in. And within this system, the story was always told the same way: "You are a sinner. You are broken. You are unworthy. Accept Jesus so God won't punish you." Even when framed gently, the underlying tone was guilt, fear, and inadequacy. This version of the Gospel deeply shaped how I once read Scripture, how I understood God, and how I saw myself.

Then came 2020. This is the year we all remember as the beginning and height of the COVID-19 Pandemic. But for me, this was the start of a challenging time in life. After my 2017 and 2020 books took off, after signing multiple new academic contracts between 2019 and 2021, something in me collapsed. I hit a wall I didn't expect. My career was moving in a direction that I'd dreamed it would when I set down this path two decades earlier. I had reputable publications, speaking invites and engagements, academic teaching offers. But something inside me wasn't right. And my success was quickly overwhelmed by anxiety, depression, loss of purpose—all the things I could analyze on paper became unmanageable when I felt them in my own bones. I kept teaching, kept reading, kept showing up. But internally, it felt as if I were wrestling with something I couldn't name, couldn't subdue, couldn't outthink.

In a strange and unsettling way, it felt like I was living inside Romans 7. That Paul's cries for rescue from his own members was *my* cry, too. I had always treated those verses as exegetical puzzles. Suddenly, they felt like autobiography. And that's when the scholarly work and my personal struggle collided with each other.

My research and publications on divine embodiment, ancient indwelling, porous selves, monstrous origins, and chaos myths—along with my background in Jesus, Paul, and the New Testament—began illuminating Paul's language in new ways. Meanwhile, my work on Jesus—particularly his role as the storm-stiller, the chaos-tamer, the one who confronts the monstrous forces (Sea, Storm, Legion, Death)—pushed me to see the Gospels themselves as cosmic warfare narratives.

And slowly, a new picture emerged: Sin and Death are not metaphors. They are invasive powers. They are cosmic forces operating like possessing agents. And salvation is not about moral repair—it is about eviction and indwelling. It is habitation, not behavior. It is liberation, not shame.

Once I saw it, I couldn't unsee it.

Everything converged—my academic work on embodiment, my childhood fascination with the monstrous, my study of chaos-beings in Scripture, my re-examination of the Gospel, and my own internal struggles that felt like possession more than temptation. Paul's anthropology suddenly fit perfectly within the mythic logic of the ancient world: humans are contested space—temples, houses, bodies designed for occupancy.

And Jesus is the stronger occupant. The invader who evicts the invaders. The holy monster who meets the monstrous powers on their own territory and overturns them from within.

That is where this book came from. A convergence of the intellectual and the personal. A long wrestling match with forces ancient and modern. An attempt to understand not just Paul's theology, but my own life.

And here is what I need you to know: this book offers a different model—a theological, exegetical, and existential alternative to the shame-based Gospel many of us inherited. It reframes Sin and Death not as moral stains but as occupying powers; salvation not as avoidance of punishment but as divine indwelling; Jesus not as moral instructor but as cosmic liberator; and humanity not as worthless sinners but as sacred architecture reclaimed by God.

In other words, this is not just a new way of reading Paul. It is a new way of reading ourselves. A new way of understanding what is broken, what is possible, and what the Gospel truly announces.

You may find that this book unsettles you at times. It should. To speak truthfully about Sin and Death is to name the monsters that theology has often tamed into abstractions. But there is hope in that honesty. The monsters are real, yes—but they are not sovereign. They are powerful, but not ultimate. The Gospel does not deny their reality. It declares their defeat.

Nikos Kazantzakis's Christ, at war within himself, as captured in the quote in the previous section of this book, embodies what Paul saw in all of us: the fierce longing of flesh and spirit to be reconciled. The Incarnation is that longing fulfilled—the divine entering the human not to escape it, but to reclaim it. That is the scandal and the beauty of the Christian story: God does not annihilate the monster; he inhabits the body it haunts and drives it out from within.

This is the story I want to retell—not small, moralistic religion, but a cosmic drama of possession and liberation. It is about haunted humanity and divine indwelling, about the monsters that rule us and the Christ who overthrows them. It is about the human soul as arena, the body as temple, and the Gospel as the thunder that shakes the walls of both.

The dual substance of Christ, Kazantzakis said, opened in him "large wounds and also large flowing springs." I suspect it will do the same for us.

If it does—good. That means the battle has begun, and perhaps, the healing, too.

And for me, that's the key. The healing. Because understanding the Gospel as it really is should be liberating, not damning; healing, not harming; a moment of peace, not fear.

God did not come to battle against *you*, but he came to set you free from the suffocating grip of Sin and Death. You are not his enemy. Sin and Death are.

In the pages that follow, I hope to re-present the Gospel not as a story of guilt and shame, but as a story of deliverance—a story in which the monsters that haunt us are named, confronted, and overthrown by a love far stronger than their power to destroy. I'll present a host of ancient texts that you've probably never heard of, and all translations of non-biblical and biblical texts are my own—part of my aim to provide you a completely fresh look at Scripture and the Gospel story. And to the peer reviewers who carefully, and sometimes frighteningly, critiqued this book I owe enormous thanks.

If the old story left you afraid, ashamed, or exhausted, this book is my attempt to show you a different one—one where the powers fall, the haunted house is reclaimed, and the Spirit moves back in. Where the Gospel is not guilt, but glory. Not fear, but freedom. Not accusation, but inhabitation.

And where, for the first time, you might finally breathe.

*LEKH ULMAD*—Go and Learn.

Tyson

# TABLE OF CONTENTS

# CHAPTER 1—INTRODUCTION

## RETHINKING THE GOSPEL STORY

Christians have long told the Gospel as a story of guilt and pardon. Humanity sins, God judges, Christ intervenes, forgiveness is granted. This framework has shaped preaching, catechesis, and personal faith for centuries. It offers clarity, moral seriousness, and a sense of resolution. It is also deeply familiar to most readers.

But familiarity is not the same as faithfulness.

When the Gospel is reduced primarily to a legal exchange, the biblical story becomes smaller than the Scriptures themselves. The drama of creation, corruption, and restoration is narrowed into a private transaction between God and the individual conscience. Salvation becomes a solution to guilt rather than a rescue from captivity. The language of Scripture—thick with conflict, struggle, invasion, and deliverance—gets flattened into moral accounting.

Across Christian traditions, this narrowing takes different forms. In some, salvation is framed sacramentally; in others, morally; in others, juridically. Each approach captures something real. Yet all of them risk sidelining a more fundamental biblical concern: the condition of humanity itself and the forces that deform it.

The Bible does not begin by asking, "How can guilty individuals be forgiven?" It begins by asking, "What has gone wrong with creation, with humanity, and with life itself?" It tells a story in which human beings are not merely rule-breakers, but participants in a world that has come under hostile influence—where life is distorted, relationships are fractured, and death exercises real power. The problem is not only what humans do, but what has happened to them.

In other words, the Bible's story is not built on the assumption that humans are, at their core, loathsome creatures whom God reluctantly tolerates (cf. Sanders, 1977). It does not begin with the premise that

1

humanity is fundamentally disgusting, rebellious, or deserving of divine hatred. That idea—familiar from certain strands of preaching—has shaped Christian imagination far more than many realize. But it is not the starting point of Scripture.

The biblical story begins instead with grief. Grief over a world that has been damaged. Grief over human lives bent out of shape. Grief over a creation that no longer functions as it should. The problem is not simply that people have broken God's rules; it is that something has gone wrong with us and around us. Humanity is not portrayed first as an enemy to be crushed, but as a good creation that has been wounded, misdirected, and overtaken.

This book argues that to recover the Gospel in its biblical depth, we must rethink several assumptions that often go unquestioned. We must rethink what Scripture means by sin. We must rethink what it means by death. We must rethink how the Bible understands human nature. And we must rethink what kind of salvation Christ actually brings.

Put simply, the claim of this book is this: the Gospel is not first about moral improvement or legal acquittal, but about rescue, restoration, and renewed life. Forgiveness matters, but it is not the whole story. Salvation addresses not only guilt, but bondage; not only actions, but conditions; not only behavior, but the forces that shape and constrain human existence.

This also reshapes how we understand God's anger in Scripture. God is not depicted as seething with disgust at ordinary human weakness, nor as perpetually offended by human limitation. The biblical witness consistently directs divine anger toward forces and systems that destroy life—hatred, violence, injustice, idolatry, empire, exploitation, and the powers that twist human communities into instruments of death.

God's anger is not the rage of a deity embarrassed by flawed creatures. It is the opposition of a Creator who loves his world and refuses to accept what has been done to it. Scripture's judgments are aimed not at humanity as such, but at whatever dehumanizes—at the powers that enslave, consume, and hollow people out, and at those who knowingly align themselves with those forces.

This reframing does not discard Christian tradition, nor does it deny the importance of repentance, faith, or ethical transformation. Rather, it asks whether our dominant categories have obscured elements of the biblical story that were once central. When Scripture speaks about sin, death, and salvation, it often does so in language of power, domination, and deliverance. These are not rhetorical flourishes. They reflect a worldview in which humanity is entangled in realities larger than individual moral choice.

Put even more simply: the biblical story does not say, "You are terrible, and God is furious." It says, "Something has hijacked the human story, and God has come to set it right." Human beings still bear responsibility—we make real choices, we cause real harm—but those choices take place inside a world that is already bent. The Gospel addresses that deeper reality.

This is why shame-based versions of Christianity ultimately collapse under their own weight. If the core message is that you are bad and must try harder, the result is either despair or pretense. But if the core message is that you have been caught in something larger than yourself—and that God has acted decisively to free you—then repentance becomes something very different. It becomes cooperation with healing rather than self-loathing.

The purpose of this book, then, is not to sensationalize the Gospel or to replace theology with mythology. It is to take Scripture seriously on its own terms. That means listening carefully to how biblical writers describe the human condition, how they imagine evil and corruption, and how they portray God's response—not as distant adjudication, but as active intervention.

For many readers, this reframing will feel unsettling. It may require questioning assumptions absorbed through sermons, songs, and well-intentioned teaching—assumptions about God's posture toward humanity, about what sin really is, and about what salvation is for. That discomfort is not a failure of faith. It is often the beginning of clarity.

If the Gospel has been taught primarily as a message of shame management—of trying to convince people they are bad enough to need saving—then re-examining it can feel like pulling the floor out from under everything. But what this book asks is not that readers abandon faith, only that they allow Scripture to tell its own story, even when that story is larger, stranger, and more hopeful than what they were handed.

So let me state as clearly as possible what this book is arguing. I am asking you to reconsider the Gospel story by looking again at three closely related elements that shape how it is told and heard. First, when the Bible speaks about "sin" and "death," it often does so in ways that go beyond moral failure or biological inevitability. Throughout Scripture, Sin and Death are portrayed as forces or powers. Sin crouches like a predator, clings like a burden, or contaminates like mold. Death, likewise, is not treated simply as an event but as a hostile force that devours, reigns, and resists God's creative purposes. These descriptions reflect a worldview in which God's enemies are not human beings themselves, but invading forces at work within God's good world.

Second, if Sin and Death—not humanity—are the primary enemies in this story, then the Gospel addresses something deeper than legal acquittal. Forgiveness matters, but Scripture consistently frames salvation as rescue and restoration, not merely pardon. The Gospels present Jesus not as confronting humanity as God's enemy, but as confronting the powers that have taken humanity captive. He announces the Kingdom of God as an active intrusion into occupied space. When Paul takes up this same story in Romans, he names those forces with startling precision. Sin reigns. Death rules. Salvation comes not through moral perfection, but through a change of inhabitation, as the Spirit of God takes up residence where Sin and Death once exercised control.

Third, this reframing reshapes what the Gospel means for human life before God. It does not deny responsibility for sin, but it refuses to locate the problem in human nature alone. Scripture presents human beings not as God's enemies, but as captives within a larger conflict between God and the forces that enslave creation. The result is not permission to excuse wrongdoing, but freedom from the burden of shame that assumes perfection was ever the point. The language that governs this story is not firstly courtroom language. It is the language of occupation, eviction, and renewed life—a vision that comes into its sharpest focus in Romans 5–8.

This way of reading Scripture also reshapes how we understand God's posture toward humanity. The Bible does not begin with the assumption that human beings are loathsome creatures whom God tolerates with barely concealed anger. It begins with a good creation that has been damaged, distorted, and overtaken. God's opposition in Scripture is directed primarily toward whatever destroys life, corrodes justice, and dehumanizes his creatures (cf. Wright, 2013). Sin and Death, along with the systems and practices that align with them, are the objects of divine judgment. Humanity, by contrast, is consistently portrayed as something worth rescuing, healing, and reclaiming. In this sense, God's anger is not the fury of a deity offended by weakness. It is the resistance of a creator who refuses to accept what has been done to his world.

This book therefore asks readers to reconsider what kind of story the Gospel actually is. It is not first a message designed to shame people into moral seriousness. It is an announcement that something has gone wrong at the level of life itself, and that God has acted decisively to confront and undo it. Human responsibility still matters. Choices still matter. Harm is real, and repentance is necessary. But those realities take place within a larger drama in which humanity has been caught in something it did not originate and cannot escape on its own. The Gospel addresses that deeper condition. It names the powers at work. It announces their defeat. And it proclaims the restoration of human life through the presence of God himself.

Only once that claim is made explicitly does the rest of the New Testament fall into place. What follows traces how this logic appears across the Gospels, the letters, and the apocalyptic imagination of early Christianity, before returning to Paul to examine how this drama unfolds within the human self.

Although this book reads broadly across the canon, the letters of Paul occupy a central place in the argument. This is not because Paul invents the framework described here, but because he articulates it with unusual clarity and intensity. Paul does not merely repeat Israel's language about Sin and Death. He concentrates it, internalizes it, and traces its consequences within the human self. In his letters, especially Romans, the cosmic struggle that runs through Scripture moves decisively into the body. Sin does not only corrupt the world. It dwells within the self. Death does not only mark the end of life. It exerts rule over life itself.

For that reason, Paul provides the most sustained theological account of what it means for human beings to live under occupation and what it means for that occupation to be overturned. His language of indwelling, slavery, reign, and liberation is not incidental. It is the place where the Bible's older monster grammar becomes explicit, personal, and unavoidable. This book therefore returns to Paul not to privilege him over other voices, but because his writings force the questions of sin, death, and salvation into their sharpest focus.

## THE MONSTERS ACROSS THE NEW TESTAMENT

This reframing forces a basic but often overlooked question. If the devil is not the primary enslaver of humanity in the biblical story, then who is? And what powers does the New Testament actually name as the forces that rule, occupy, and deform human life? When we step back and read across the New Testament canon, the answer is remarkably consistent. The dominant antagonists are not Satan and his demons, but the older and more pervasive powers of Sin and Death. These are the forces described as reigning, enslaving, and dwelling within human beings. They are not treated as abstractions or metaphors, but as active realities that distort agency, corrupt life, and spread their dominion across the world. Once Satan is understood as a secondary figure whose

5

influence lies primarily in deception, the New Testament's main concern comes into view with new clarity. The central problem is not a trickster at the margins, but monsters at the center. Sin and Death are the powers that inhabit human flesh, and they are the powers the Gospel announces have been confronted and defeated.

To see this more clearly, we need to look across the New Testament canon—not simply at Paul, but at the Gospels, Hebrews, Revelation, and the broader apostolic writings. When we do, a consistent grammar emerges: the human crisis is not just moral failure or spiritual confusion but cosmic captivity. The world is under occupation. Human beings are not independent agents navigating moral choices but creatures caught in a struggle of rival indwellers—one destructive, one life-giving. Evil in the New Testament is not simply a matter of temptation; it is a matter of tenancy.

### The Gospels: Exorcism as the Shape of Salvation

The story begins with Jesus himself. In the Synoptic Gospels, the first public act of Jesus' campaign is not preaching but exorcism (Mark 1:21–28). Before he ever calls disciples or teaches crowds, he confronts a force that has entered a human body and taken over its speech. The unclean spirit cries out, "I know who you are—the Holy One of God!" (v. 24). Demons recognize Jesus before the crowds do. They sense the arrival of a rival power. Jesus' very presence destabilizes them. The Kingdom of God is an invasion.

This, in miniature, reveals how the Gospels frame salvation. Jesus does not primarily offer moral advice or philosophical insight. He evicts. He reclaims. Every healing, every exorcism, every confrontation with an unclean spirit is a sign that God has begun to repossess what has long been occupied. Mark 3:27 makes the theology explicit: first bind the strong man, then plunder his house. The world—and the human body—is assumed to be a haunted place, and Jesus is the stronger intruder reclaiming it.

The Gerasene demoniac (Mark 5:1–13) pushes this imagery further. The Legion occupying the man is not a psychological metaphor but a collective entity with its own will. They ask for relocation into swine, a grotesque mimicry of incarnation. The herd rushes into the sea, the ancient symbol of chaos, as if the demons recognize their ancestral home. The point is not simply that Jesus has power over demons, but that his mission announces the collapse of a cosmic occupation.

### John: Death as Tyrant, Sin as Master

The Gospel of John reframes the same truth with a different angle. John rarely focuses on exorcisms, but he intensifies the personal agency of evil. Jesus declares, "Everyone who commits sin is a slave of Sin" (John 8:34). That line is worth hearing in slow motion. Sin is not just something humans do; Sin is a master whose slaves do its will. John later merges this power with Death itself, calling the devil "a murderer from the beginning" (John 8:44). The target of Jesus' ministry, then, is not merely ignorance or doubt—it is bondage to a murderous force that holds humanity captive.

The raising of Lazarus in John 11 brings this into sharper focus. Jesus does not approach the tomb in quiet reverence. The Greek says he snorted with anger (*embrimāomai*), a word used for the roar of a warhorse. Death is not a stage of life in John's worldview; Death is a tyrant. And Jesus stands before Lazarus's tomb not as a sentimental comforter but as a warrior who has come to tear open Death's territory. When Lazarus emerges, wrapped like cargo, it is an act of open plunder.

### Hebrews: Liberation from Death

Hebrews sets the drama on a cosmic stage: "That through Death he might destroy the one who has the power of Death, that is, the devil" (Hebrews 2:14–15). Death is a tyrant who wields fear as a weapon. The devil appears here, but his role is custodial. He holds the weapon; he does not originate the power. Death itself is the deeper enslaver. And the incarnation is portrayed not as a sentimental act of solidarity but as a tactical invasion: Christ becomes killable so that he can enter Death's domain from the inside and break it open.

### Revelation: The Monsters Resurface and Meet Their End

Revelation gathers up all the strands. The chaos-beasts of the Hebrew Bible reappear in grand apocalyptic form: the dragon (Revelation 12), the beast from the sea (13:1), the beast from the land (13:11). These monsters amplify imperial and cosmic evil, but at the climax of the book it is not Satan who is the final enemy destroyed. It is Death and Hades (Revelation 20:14). They are the last powers thrown into the lake of fire. The final victory of God is not over a devil with horns but over the ancient devourer and the underworld that sustains it.

## Paul: The Invasion Within

Paul takes the Gospel's cosmic drama and moves it inside the human body. In Romans he names the forces that oppress humanity with almost clinical precision: Sin entered (5:12). Death spread (5:12). Sin reigned (5:21). Death ruled (5:14). These verbs do not belong to psychological tendencies. They belong to agents—powers with their own activity and intent. Paul speaks of Sin as if it walks, grasps, and seizes opportunity (Romans 7:8, 11). He describes Death as a monarch (Romans 5:14) and as "the last enemy" to be destroyed (1 Corinthians 15:26). Modern readers tend to soften this language, but Paul's first-century audience would not have. They knew the grammar of personified cosmic powers from Israel's Scriptures and from the mythic imagination of the ancient Near East.

What makes Paul distinctive is how interior this battle becomes. Sin does not merely rule the world—it "dwells in me" (Romans 7:17, 20). The human body has become contested territory. Paul's anthropology assumes that the self is porous, habitable, and vulnerable to invasion—an assumption inherited from the spatial logic of ancient anthropology. In Romans 7, these powers take up residence in the self and hijack human agency: "What I hate, I do... it is no longer I who do it, but Sin dwelling in me" (7:15–20). Whether Paul speaks autobiographically or representatively, the point stands: this is the language of occupation, not mere temptation.

And the only hope, as Romans 8 declares, is a stronger indweller—"the Spirit of God who dwells in you" (8:9–11). Salvation, in Paul's imagination, is not a verdict. It is an eviction and a reoccupation. What the Gospels depict externally in Jesus' exorcisms, Paul describes internally: the Spirit dispossessing the forces that once ruled the body and reclaiming the self as divine space.

## A Unified Grammar of Evil

Read together, the New Testament's voices form a consistent pattern. The human problem is not framed primarily in terms of guilt or moral failure but in terms of cosmic bondage. Sin deceives (Romans 7:11), enslaves (John 8:34), and dwells within (Romans 7:17–20). Death reigns (Romans 5:14), tyrannizes (Hebrews 2:14–15), and devours (1 Corinthians 15:54). Satan deceives, but he does not occupy. Demons disrupt, but they do not reign. Throughout the canon, Sin and Death are the central antagonists—the monsters that rule the old creation and inhabit human flesh.

8

This is the backdrop for the Gospel's announcement: the stronger one has come. Christ has overthrown their rule, reclaimed the human self for God, and begun the long work of reconstituting humanity from the inside out. This is why the New Testament speaks with such embodied, almost mythic realism. The earliest Christians were not describing moral impulses but invasive powers. And the salvation they proclaimed was not merely forgiveness. It was liberation. It was repossession. It was the restoration of divine habitation in a world—and in bodies—that had been occupied by rival powers.

What this survey shows is not a collection of isolated metaphors, but a shared way of seeing the human condition. Across the New Testament, Sin and Death are treated as real powers that invade, inhabit, and rule. The Gospel is announced as God's response to that invasion. Christ does not come primarily to improve human behavior or to settle a legal account. He comes to confront the forces that have taken hold of humanity and to reclaim human life from within. The chapters that follow will trace this story in detail. We will examine how Sin and Death are imagined as living powers, how they come to occupy the human self, and how the Gospel proclaims not merely forgiveness, but liberation, reoccupation, and restored life. Only when we see the problem clearly can we understand why the solution takes the form it does.

## OVERVIEW OF THE BOOK'S STRUCTURE AND GOALS

If Paul's writings reveal a self haunted by rival indwellers and reclaimed by the Spirit of Christ, then the task before us is clear: we must trace how this drama came to be and how Scripture invites us to understand our own humanity within it. In order to demonstrate this, the chapters that follow move outward and backward—outward into the cosmic landscape of Sin and Death, and backward into the ancient worlds that gave these beings shape. Only then can we return to Paul with the clarity his arguments require.

This book unfolds in seven chapters and an epilogue, each building toward a unified vision of the human person as sacred space contested by monstrous powers and repossessed by Christ.

*Chapter 2, The Monstrous Framework*, establishes the conceptual world we must inhabit to read Scripture on its own terms. Here, I explore what "monster" means in ancient literature—why beings that violate boundaries, blend categories, or dwell in liminal zones were understood as threats to cosmic order. Ancient Near Eastern myths did not picture monsters as mindless beasts; they were quasi-divine agents, embodiments of chaos, often descended from the gods themselves. By recovering this ancient grammar, we gain a vocabulary for reading Sin and Death not as metaphors but as beings who fit the monstrous profile.

*Chapter 3, Death as a Living Monster*, turns directly to the figure of Mōt and the biblical imagination shaped by him. The Hebrew Bible presents Death as a devouring force: opening its appetite wide (Isaiah 5:14), spreading snares (Psalm 18:5), swallowing cities and nations whole. This chapter maps the ancient logic that made Death the great predator of creation and shows why early Christians understood Christ's resurrection as a direct assault on that predator's dominion.

*Chapter 4, Sin as a Living Monster*, parallels my arguments about Death by exploring how ancient peoples depicted "sin" not as a moral misstep but as a contaminating, invasive presence. From the crouching creature of Genesis 4:7 to Paul's description of Sin "dwelling in me" (Romans 7:17–20), this chapter traces a cross-cultural pattern: Sin behaves like an entity with its own desires, its own agency, and its own will to dominate. What most modern readers dissolve into psychology, ancient texts treat as a spiritual invader.

*Chapter 5, Monstrous Humanity in Romans 5–8*, is the exegetical center of the book. Here, I show, text by text, how Paul draws on these ancient categories to portray humanity not as morally weak but as ontologically occupied. Romans 5 introduces Sin and Death as the two great rulers of the old creation. Romans 6 describes their mastery over human members. Romans 7 gives voice to the horror of that mastery from within. This chapter argues that Paul is not describing guilt but possession, not moral struggle but rival tenancy. This chapter then turns to Romans 8 to look at how Paul frames the return of the rightful Lord. Paul deliberately mirrors his earlier language—Sin "dwells," and now the Spirit "dwells." Sin "reigns," and now the Spirit "gives life." This chapter shows how Paul envisions salvation as a change of occupancy, a divine re-indwelling that renovates the self from the inside out and begins the slow reconstruction of human nature.

*Chapter 6, Our Monstrous Lord and Savior Jesus Christ*, turns the framework inside out. If Sin and Death are monstrous in the older mythic sense, then Christ is the stronger monster—holy, hybrid, terrifying to the powers, unkillable. This chapter argues that Christ fulfills the logic of ancient monster stories but inverts their purpose. He does not threaten creation—he threatens its tyrants. His resurrection is the moment the devourer is devoured. And because he indwells his people, his monstrous life becomes theirs.

*Chapter 7, Conclusion: The Haunted Made Holy*, then draws all of the theological threads together. If the human self is sacred space and if Sin and Death are real occupiers, then Christian anthropology cannot remain a matter of guilt and moral effort. It must be rethought in terms of possession and liberation. "Sin management," as many modern Christians practice it, does not address the real crisis. The Gospel does. Christ does. The Spirit does. This chapter reframes Christian life not as behavior modification but as ongoing re-sanctification of the self by the indwelling Christ.

*Epilogue, What All of This Means: Gospel, Not Shame*, speaks plainly to the pastoral stakes of this project. Many Christians live under a crushing burden of guilt, convinced that their failures have led God to carry a fiery anger toward them. But if Paul is right—and if Scripture's monsters are taken seriously—then the problem is not that humans are fundamentally bad, but that we are fundamentally inhabited, occupied. The Gospel, then, is not a story about shaming the self but about naming the monsters and proclaiming their defeat.

*Appendix: Resituating Satan in the Biblical Drama* seeks to answer questions about Satan that inevitably arise in any discussion of evil and cosmic conflict. Thus, this book also includes a brief appendix devoted specifically to that topic. The purpose of the appendix is not to elevate the devil to a central role he does not occupy in the biblical texts, but to clarify how he functions within the wider framework traced throughout the book. By treating this question separately, the main argument is able to remain focused on the powers that Scripture consistently places at the center of the human crisis—Sin and Death—while still offering readers a clear, textually grounded account of where the devil fits, and where he does not.

This introduction is the doorway to a new and haunting world for many of you. The chapters ahead trace the contours of a world we have never quite been taught to see—a world where the human self stands at the center of a cosmic struggle, where Sin and Death are not metaphors but invaders, and where Christ comes not to scold but to save, not to wag a finger but to win a war.

# CHAPTER 2—THE MONSTROUS FRAMEWORK

## DEFINING THE MONSTER

To understand humanity's monstrous nature, we must first understand what a monster is. This idea, in both ancient and modern thought, is never neutral. It signals transgression—of bodies, of boundaries, of being itself. And in the world of the Bible and its ancient Near Eastern neighbors, monsters were hardly fictional—they were theological, and for the ancients, they were real (cf. Dalley, 2000).

When I use the word "monster" here, I do not mean "evil" in the narrow, moral sense we often assign to it today. In modern usage, monsters are almost always villains—malevolent forces or beings bent on destruction. But in the ancient imagination, monstrosity was not a synonym for wickedness. It described a condition of being: boundary-breaking, category-defying, world-disrupting (Asma, 2009; Cohen, 1996; Beal, 2022). Thus, a monster could be terrifying without being "morally bad." Monstrosity was about transgression of order, not ethics (Cohen, 1996). This distinction is crucial, because it allows us to see how figures like Sin, Death, Chaos, and even Christ himself can be called "monstrous" without collapsing the category into simple notions of good and evil. In fact, the Bible itself presents "holy monsters" (Hamori, 2023). Think of the fiery seraphim of Isaiah's vision (Isaiah 6:2–4) or the hybrid, many-faced creatures of Ezekiel's throne vision (Ezekiel 1:4–14). These beings are unsettling, boundary-crossing, destructive, and fearsome, but they are not evil. They reveal God's glory and otherness precisely through their own *otherness*.

In ancient myth, monsters functioned not as fantasy creatures but as divine anomalies. They were not simply "other" in some abstract sense—they were dangerous deviations from the divine order. Tiamat, the primordial sea goddess in Babylonian myth, births monsters from her own body—dragons, serpents, and hybrid horrors—after being betrayed by the younger gods. She is not an evil caricature. She is divine chaos in grotesque, living form (Dalley, 2000). Mōt, the god of Death in Ugaritic myth, is not a metaphor but a divine being whose very hunger undoes creation (Smith, 2001; Pardee, 2002). Leviathan in Job and Isaiah is not a mere sea creature—it is a chaos creature whom only YHWH can subdue (Job 41:1–34; Isaiah 27:1; Day, 1985).

These ancient figures reflect a theology of threat. A monster is not just scary—it is dangerous to existence. It threatens the very possibility of divine order. Thus, when we speak of monsters in biblical and ancient Near Eastern texts, we are not speaking about Halloween costumes or mythological curiosities. We are speaking of beings whose existence challenges the cosmos.

## MONSTERS AS REFLECTIONS OF THE HUMAN SELF

If monsters are not merely physical anomalies but theological and symbolic beings, then their meaning lies not only in what they *are* but in what they *reveal*. One of the most enduring insights of modern monster theory is that monsters are mirrors (Beal, 2022; Cohen, 1996). They are projections of the hidden, the repressed, the feared parts of our own selves. And this is not just a modern insight. The Bible and ancient texts often reflect this same pattern: the monster is out there, but also disturbingly familiar. We see it—and we see ourselves (Beal, 2022).

The monster, in many ways, represents what Sigmund Freud famously called the uncanny (*das Unheimliche*). In his 1919 essay by that title, translated as "The Uncanny," Freud defined the concept of the uncanny as follows:

> The subject of the uncanny ... undoubtedly belongs to all that is terrible—to all that arouses dread and creeping horror (p. 1).

> The "uncanny" is that class of the terrifying which leads back to something long known to us, once very familiar ... circumstances [in which] the familiar can become uncanny and frightening (pp. 2-3).

> [T]his uncanny is in reality nothing new or foreign, but something familiar and old—established in the mind that has been estranged only through the process of repression (p. 13).

Literally, the German term *un-heimlich* means "un-homelike." The *heimlich* is what is intimate, safe, domestic—the space of belonging. Its negation—the *unheimlich*—evokes what *should* be familiar but feels disturbingly foreign. The uncanny, then, is the moment when the home turns hostile, when the ordinary reveals something disquietingly strange beneath its surface. It is the feeling that something once trusted has become unstable, that what should shelter us is instead watching us.

Freud's insight is that this disturbance arises not from encountering true otherness but from confronting what has always been ours—some buried piece of selfhood suddenly made visible. The uncanny is unsettling not because it is wholly alien but because it is too close. It is what we have repressed, returning to the surface in a form we no longer recognize. "In reality," Freud writes, "nothing new or foreign, but something familiar and old—established in the mind that has been estranged only through the process of repression" (Freud, 1919, p. 13). The monster, in this sense, is the return of what we tried to bury—the estranged homecoming of our own darkness.

Anthropologically, this insight runs deep. The uncanny may arise from primordial memory, the faint echo of a more primal self—the ancient animal within us that survived by aggression, predation, and fear. In the modern world, that monstrous inheritance rarely finds legitimate expression. Yet it remains within the psyche, repressed but alive. When we encounter violence or monstrosity—whether on a screen, in history, or in ourselves—we are startled not only by its horror but by its familiarity. Something in us recognizes it.

In theological terms, the uncanny is a kind of spiritual déjà vu. It is the moment we sense that the monster we dread is not *out there* but *in here*. As Freud observed, the uncanny "is that class of terrifying that leads back to something long known to us" (Freud, 1919, pp. 2–3). The ancient serpent, the crouching beast at Cain's door, the Sin that "dwells within"—these are biblical portraits of the same phenomenon. The monstrous is terrifying precisely because it reintroduces us to a part of ourselves we thought was gone.

As Marina Levina and Diem-My T. Bui explain:

> The uncanny is a kind of haunting proximity. The psychoanalytical approach thus perceives the monster as that which used to be a part of the self and needed to be cast away in order for the self to become unified or, at least, functional. Thus an encounter with the monster reminds the self of what it has lost (Levina and Bui, 2013, p. 3).

This is the paradox at the heart of monstrosity: the monster is the exiled self. It is the piece of our being we have disowned, the shadow we cast when we stand before the light. The monster is not born in distant swamps or infernal realms—it is born in us. We are the cave from which it emerges and the house it haunts.

In this book's theological frame, that insight becomes literal. The uncanny is not only psychological but ontological. Humanity itself is the site of divine and monstrous inhabitation—the house divided. The Pauline language of "indwelling" (*oikeō*) and haunting gives the uncanny its biblical body: Sin lives in me, and the Spirit lives in me (Gaventa, 2011; 2016; 2024; Wright, 2013). The home of the self is both *heimlich* and *unheimlich*—a dwelling of both divine and desecrated.

The monster terrifies us because it is us. The study of the monster, therefore, is always a study of the self. And in the present work, our search for monsters in the ancient world—Mōt, Tiamat, Leviathan, Sin, and Death—is also a search for the monstrous within humanity itself: the haunted house that is our own flesh, the uncanny temple where God and chaos still contend.

Monsters terrify precisely because they are both near and not-near, like a distorted reflection of ourselves. This is why the most disturbing monsters are not always aliens or beasts but those that blur into our own humanity—zombies, vampires, or as I'll show, the "possessed self" of Romans 5–7.

Think of Dr. Jekyll and Mr. Hyde, or Gollum in Tolkien's *Lord of the Rings*, or even Bruce Banner and the Incredible Hulk. These figures are not just *invaded by* monsters—they *become* them. Their monstrosity emerges from within, exposing the instability of identity itself. Jekyll's scientific ambition unearths a darker Hyde. Gollum's obsession with the Ring mutates him into a wraith of himself. Banner's rage erupts as the Hulk, uncontrollable and destructive. In each case, the monster is a psychological double, an alter ego born from the cracks in the self.

Monsters, as Timothy Beal puts it, are meaning machines that reflect cultural anxieties and expose the cracks in our social and spiritual frameworks (Beal, 2022). Jeffrey Jerome Cohen argues that the monster's body is a type of cultural body, a projection of what a society fears and represses (Cohen, 1996). Brandon Grafius sharpens this for biblical interpretation: monsters in Scripture function as mirrors, reflecting what we fear within ourselves when boundaries collapse (Grafius, 2018). Esther Hamori likewise shows that biblical monsters are not random curiosities but meaningful beings—hybrids, chaos creatures, and transgressive figures that reveal theological anxieties in Israel's world (Hamori, 2023). Monsters are projections of internal fractures onto an external canvas. Pharaoh in Exodus, for instance, is not just a tyrant but a monster of the Nile (Ezekiel 29:3), embodying Israel's deepest fear of bondage and disorder. Goliath, towering over

Israel's army, is less an individual giant than a mirror of Israel's own cowardice and wavering faith. The monster stands outside but also reveals the fracture inside.

Safwat Marzouk, analyzing Egypt and its role in the Hebrew Bible, makes the same point. The monstrous imagery used to describe Egypt is not only polemical but reflective: Israel's portrayal of the other exposes its own anxieties about disobedience, identity, and survival (Marzouk, 2015). To call Egypt a dragon or a monster is to project Israel's own fractures outward, externalizing what it cannot face directly.

Monsters, in short, are symbolic scapegoats for what we fear most in ourselves. We place our chaos *out there*—in demons, dragons, or enemies—because we do not want to recognize it *in here*. Yet Scripture does not let us escape so easily. Paul collapses the categories when he writes that Sin itself lives in him (Romans 7:17). The monster is not only at the gates, but it is inside the walls. To grapple with the monstrous is to admit that the enemy is not only the *other*—it is also *us* (Beal, 2022).

Taken together, these perspectives remind us that monstrosity is not about moral categories but about transgression. Monsters live at the cracks where categories fray—neither fully human nor fully animal, neither fully alive nor fully dead, neither fully god nor fully mortal. They appear at thresholds and in liminal spaces, forcing us to face the instability of the systems we thought kept our world intact. In this sense, modern monster theory returns us to the same realization that haunted the ancient imagination: monstrosity is about what happens when the boundaries that hold the world together come undone.

## CONSTRUCTING THE FRAMEWORK

Monstrosity, then, is not simply the grotesque. It is breach—those moments when creation's borders fail and something other crosses the threshold. To work responsibly with this idea, I need to clarify what I mean by "monster" and "the monstrous," and why this matters for the chapters ahead.

Rather than treating monsters as a fixed category, I approach them through traits (Cohen, 1996; Asma, 2009; Beal, 2022). The literature on monstrosity—psychological, anthropological, mythological—identifies recurring patterns by which cultures recognize something or someone as monstrous. A "true" monster tends to display several of these traits at once, though not always in the same proportions. Size, for instance, may amplify monstrosity but is not essential to it. What matters is the constellation of attributes that signals a being has crossed a line it was never meant to cross.

I am also interested in beings who may not be monsters in the strictest sense yet nevertheless exhibit a significant number of these same traits. By identifying the core features that make monsters monstrous, we can broaden the field of ancient Near Eastern and biblical discourse to include entities often overlooked in discussions of mythic or theological monstrosity.

What follows, then, is a framework built from five traits. They are not rigid categories but overlapping dimensions—an attempt to deconstruct the monster and to ask what gives rise to its identity, its presence, and its unsettling power. These traits provide the lens through which I will later examine figures like Sin and Death, whose nature becomes clearer when viewed against the backdrop of this broader theoretical vocabulary.

Let's look now at the five monstrous traits, followed by the three functions of monstrosity.

## Monstrous Trait 1—Hybridity

Monsters are boundary-breakers. They combine what should remain separate. They cross boundaries, collapse categories, and terrify precisely because they refuse to be one thing. In the ancient world, this was often the essence of monstrosity. The Minotaur of Greek myth, neither man nor beast but both, was born of divine meddling and human disobedience, a grotesque hybrid confined to the labyrinth. The Nephilim of Genesis 6, echoing wider ancient Near Eastern traditions, embody another troubling mix: the offspring of "the sons of God" and "the daughters of humans," figures whose divine-human hybridity unsettled Israel's imagination. In Babylonian myth, Tiamat's hybridity reaches another level—she is mother and monster, horrific, dragonlike creature, and the chaotic sea itself, birthing gods in her womb even as she spawns serpents, dragons, and chaos-beasts in her rage (Dalley, 2000; Putthoff, 2020). What terrifies about Tiamat is not just her violence but her refusal to stay in one category: she is at once maternal and monstrous, creative and destructive.

The Bible itself frames humanity in these terms, not as a neat category but as a hybrid being by design: "formed from the dust of the ground" and animated with "the breath of life" (Genesis 2:7). To be human is already to be a boundary-breaking being, bridging earth and heaven, matter and spirit. Yet when this delicate balance is hijacked by cosmic invaders like Sin and Death, the hybrid turns grotesque. Paul captures this in Romans 7 when he confesses, "It is no longer I who do it, but Sin dwelling in me" (7:17). We'll deal more with this in the following chapters. But as we'll see, humanity is not just morally weak. It is ontologically crossed, invaded by powers that distort its hybrid nature (Gaventa, 2011; 2024). Other biblical monsters reflect this, too. Leviathan, described in Job 41 and Isaiah 27:1, is part sea creature, part chaos deity, part symbol of all that resists divine order. He terrifies precisely because he is not one thing but many, collapsing natural and supernatural categories into a single, boundary-breaking body.

Contemporary literature and cinema still play with this same unsettling dynamic (Cohen, 1996; Asma, 2009; Beal, 2022). Mary Shelley's *Frankenstein* (1818) gave us a creature assembled from corpses and animated by human ambition—neither fully alive nor fully dead, neither natural nor unnatural. Ridley Scott's Xenomorph in *Alien* (1979) horrifies for similar reasons: insect and reptile, machine-like and organic, human-hosted yet alien-born. Zombies terrify us by collapsing the line between life and death, the living-dead who refuse to stay put in either category. And then there is Venom—my favorite comic book figure as a child (and still today!)—the Marvel anti-hero who is both alien symbiote and human host. His monstrosity is possession itself: two beings inhabiting one body, their fusion blurring the boundary between autonomy and invasion, heroism and chaos. For many, Venom embodies the nightmare of losing control to a darker presence inside. But he also fascinates, because he reveals the strange possibilities of hybrid identity, and he also shows a side of monstrosity that is not altogether evil. We'll talk more about Venom later.

Theologically, this means that hybridity itself is not evil—humans were made hybrid (Putthoff, 2020). The danger arises when that hybridity is co-opted by malign powers. When Sin and Death corrupt the divine element within us—even though God deemed our originally created self "good"—our hybrid existence becomes monstrous. The result is not just a human who errs morally but a creature who embodies *both* the divine presence *and* chaotic invasion at once. In other words, theological monstrosity is what happens when humanity's designed hybridity collapses under the weight of occupation by external, malicious forces.

## Monstrous Trait 2—Supernatural Ancestry

In many myths, monsters are not merely freak accidents of nature—they are born from the divine realm. They often carry divine blood, divine origin, or divine sanction. Tiamat, the primordial sea goddess of

Babylonian myth, does not just embody chaos. She bears it, giving birth to dragons, serpents, and hybrid horrors who fight on her behalf (Dalley, 2000). The Nephilim of Genesis 6:1–4 emerge from unions between the "sons of God" and the "daughters of humans." Their very existence blurs heaven and earth, divine and mortal. Humbaba, the grotesque forest guardian in the *Epic of Gilgamesh*, is appointed by the gods themselves, yet his figure is monstrous, ambiguous, and terrifying (George, 2003). In later Jewish apocalyptic imagination, Leviathan and Behemoth are likewise portrayed not as accidents of creation but as creatures birthed or preserved by God himself, embodiments of pre-creation chaos waiting to be revealed and destroyed (*1 Enoch* 60:7–8). The common thread is this: monsters often come from heaven (Smith, 2001). They are not aberrations of nature but corruptions of divinity, reminders that what is divine is not always benevolent.

This is a crucial theological insight. If, as I've shown in previous books (Putthoff, 2017, 2020), divine embodiment is indeed a real phenomenon—if gods indwell human bodies—then it follows that not every god or divine entity who inhabits is the God of justice or love. The biblical witness itself warns that lesser "powers," *archai* and *exousiai* in Paul's language (Romans 8:38; Colossians 2:15), can also invade, possess, and lay claim to human flesh. This flips our instinctive assumption: to be inhabited by something "divine" is not necessarily a blessing, as we in Western tradition assume. It may well be a curse.

Contemporary culture continues to explore this motif. Bram Stoker's *Dracula* (1897) horrifies precisely because Dracula's vampiric nature is both parasitic and quasi-divine—he's immortal, transcendent, unkillable by ordinary means. Tolkien's Orcs, born of Elves who've been twisted by dark powers, are monsters because their supernatural ancestry is corrupted at its root. And modern cinema gives us countless examples of hybrids with tainted lineage: from Voldemort in *Harry Potter*, conceived under a love potion and thus incapable of love, to Anakin Skywalker in *Star Wars*, "the Chosen One" whose extraordinary origin is overshadowed by his corruption into Darth Vader. Each reflects the same truth: monsters are often terrifying because they are born not from below, but from above.

### Monstrous Trait 3—Terror and Disorder

Monsters do not simply evoke fear—they cause ontological collapse. They don't just attack individual bodies, but they unmake worlds. In biblical language, this is *tōhū wābōhū*—"formless and void" (Genesis 1:2). Creation in biblical lore is less concerned with bringing new things into existence as it is with bringing order to primordial chaos (Walton, 2009; 2011). Chaos or disorder was the primal "enemy," as it were, of God and his celestial entourage. To encounter a monster is therefore to feel creation sliding back toward uncreation. When Leviathan writhes, creation shakes, when Death opens its mouth, the land itself mourns (Isaiah 5:14). These figures embody uncreation. They dissolve the distinctions that make life possible: life versus death, order versus disorder, God versus not-God. The terror of monstrosity is not that it kills, but that it undoes the fabric of reality.

Ancient myth is filled with such figures. The Ugaritic god Mōt does not simply kill. He devours indiscriminately, swallowing gods and mortals alike, threatening the very stability of the cosmos. Tiamat's rage in the *Enuma Elish* unleashes serpents, dragons, and storm-beasts that overwhelm the younger gods, threatening to return everything to watery chaos. Humbaba, in the *Epic of Gilgamesh*, terrifies not only because of his grotesque visage, but because his presence signals the collapse of safe boundaries: the forest that should be life-giving becomes a realm of dread. These beings don't merely fight—they disrupt the ordering work of creation itself.

This is why monsters remain so enduring in culture. They have a way of dramatizing our fear not only of destruction but of disorder. Godzilla is terrifying not just because he destroys cities but because he renders human control meaningless. The Xenomorph in *Alien* is horrifying because it violates the deepest boundaries of the body, turning reproduction into grotesque parasitism. And Dracula—perhaps the most iconic monster of them all—is terrifying not only because he kills but because he collapses boundaries we depend on: life and death, sacred and profane, the erotic and the violent. He stalks the night as both corpse and predator, nobleman and beast, guest and invader—all at once, and he sleeps in a coffin. As Stoker insists, he is more than man but less than divine (*Dracula*, 1897). His very existence is a parody of creation, a walking form of uncreation.

Even figures like the Joker in modern comics and cinema embody this monstrous terror. He horrifies not simply because he kills but because he makes no sense. He lives to mock the very possibility of meaning, exposing the fragility of moral order. Like the Canaanite god Mōt ("Death"), the Israelite figure Leviathan ("chaos serpent"), and the biblical Sin and Death, the Joker embodies the terrifying truth that chaos lurks just beneath the surface of existence, threatening to erupt at any moment, even when—or perhaps, *especially* when—there is no rational explanation for it.

## Monstrous Trait 4—Liminality

Monsters live on thresholds. They haunt deserts, seas, tombs, and wildernesses—places that resist easy definition. In ancient myth, Humbaba guarded the Cedar Forest, a sacred but terrifying in-between realm where the human world brushes up against the divine. Mōt ruled the underworld borderland where the living and the dead overlap. Tiamat embodied the primordial sea before land was formed, a watery Abyss poised between Creation and Chaos. These beings do not dwell in safe, ordered space. They lurk where order gives way to uncertainty.

The Bible reflects this same pattern. Demons seek "dry places" (Matthew 12:43), as though they belong not to settled land but to the in-between wastelands. Death is pictured opening its mouth in the valley (Isaiah 5:14). Jesus confronts Legion in a graveyard among swine near the edges of the Sea of Galilee (Mark 5:2–13)—a convergence of liminal zones: tombs between life and death, pigs between clean and unclean, and the sea as the ancient symbol of chaos. These encounters take place precisely where boundaries blur, where stability frays, and where monstrous forces are most at home.

The wilderness in particular is Scripture's quintessential liminal space. Israel wandered in it for forty years, between slavery and promised land, suspended between old identity and new vocation. It was there that the people were tested, fed, and reshaped. Likewise, Jesus was "driven" into the wilderness to face Satan (Mark 1:12–13; Matthew 4:1–11). This was no accident. As Victor Turner observed in his work on ritual and liminality, such spaces are "betwixt and between" (Turner, 1969)—places where categories collapse, where danger intensifies, and where transformation becomes possible. The wilderness, like the graveyard or the sea, is not neutral territory but a threshold zone, a staging ground for encounters with the monstrous and the divine alike.

Modern culture retains this instinct. Zombies terrify because they refuse to remain in one category—neither fully alive nor fully dead, endlessly wandering between states. Pennywise in Stephen King's *It* emerges from the sewer, itself a liminal space between town and underworld, and embodies liminality in his shapeshifting form: sometimes clown, sometimes beast, never stable, never one thing. Such figures frighten us not just by *what* they do but by *where* they dwell— always on the edge, eroding the boundaries that hold reality together.

Humans themselves are liminal. We are dust and breath, mortal and divine, creations who can also become beasts. Paul calls us "bodies of death" awaiting rescue (Romans 7:24). This is our monstrous paradox:

we are the temple of God and the haunted house of Death at the same time. We live at the threshold—no, we *are* the threshold—we are betwixt and between.

### Monstrous Trait 5—Persistence and Apparent Immortality

Perhaps the most unsettling feature of the monster is its refusal to die. In myth, monsters do not vanish—they recur. They may be slain, but they return with stubborn persistence, undiminished in strength. In the Ugaritic *Baal Cycle*, Mōt—the god of Death—devours Baal himself, dragging him down into the underworld. Yet when Baal rises and strikes Mōt with a sword, scattering him like chaff (KTU 1.6), the victory is only temporary. Mōt resurfaces in the next season, his hunger intact, ready to devour again. Death, it seems, cannot be killed once and for all. It always comes back (Beal, 2022).

Modern horror trades on this very motif. Michael Myers, the masked killer of John Carpenter's *Halloween* (1978), is shot, stabbed, and burned, yet he rises again in sequel after sequel, his blank face refusing to yield. Dracula, Stoker's immortal vampire, cannot be permanently destroyed. Each new telling of his story finds him returning to feed on a new generation, his undead body always one step ahead of the grave. Even in science fiction, the Xenomorph in *Alien* resists annihilation. Each time it is blasted into space or torched in fire, another egg hatches, another host is infected, and the cycle of terror begins again. The monstrous is inexhaustible. It lingers, waits, revives, and returns for more.

This is what makes monsters truly terrifying. You can destroy them, but they do not stay dead. They expose our fragile sense of finality, our illusion that victory is permanent. They are not one-time threats but recurring powers. The monstrous is that which refuses to stay buried. It keeps coming back (Beal, 2022).

### Theological Redefinition of "The Monstrous"

A monster is any being—natural or supernatural, embodied or cosmic—that resists or disrupts divine order. In the ancient world, monsters often arise from divine stock. They are not mere animals or villains. They are theological anomalies: corrupted divinity, twisted embodiment, chaotic entities born from the divine realm but now opposed to it.

And as I'll show in the following chapters, this is precisely what Sin and Death are. They are not human mistakes. They are not metaphors for bad choices. They are rogue forces—cosmic powers who possess, distort, and devour (Gaventa, 2016; 2024; Martyn, 1997). They are, in biblical terms, living, enslaving, indwelling entities. And when they take up residence in the human body, the result is monstrous.

Here, I suggest that "divine embodiment"—that is, the phenomenon in which a god or other divine entity or force indwells, inhabits, or possesses a human being—is not always a positive thing. I ask, in other words, what if not all divine embodiment is good? What if the most terrifying monsters are the ones that live in us—the ones that are not human, yet wear human skin? What if, rather than "statues" in temples, the new "idols" are our very selves, commandeered by invasive powers? As I'll show, Paul's anguished cry in Romans 7—"it is no longer I who live, but Sin who lives in me" (7:17)—is precisely this kind of possession (Gaventa, 2004; 2011; 2016; 2024). In this light, Sin and Death are not ideas about disobedience or mortality but malignant gods masquerading in human flesh.

This chapter, and the framework it provides, is the lens through which we'll examine Sin and Death—not as symbols of internal weakness, but as the monstrous offspring of heaven who have made their home in the human soul. The danger is not simply that we commit sins, and because of that, God condemns us to death. Rather, the danger—and the profundity of the Gospel—is that Sin itself has committed us and handed us over to Death. Our bodies have become their shrines, our desires their liturgy. The battle of the Gospel, therefore, is not mere moral reform but divine eviction—an exorcism in which Christ indwells where the monsters once ruled (Gaventa, 2004; 2011; 2016; 2024; Wright, 2013).

## THE THREE FUNCTIONS OF MONSTROSITY

To understand how the Bible—especially Paul—speaks of Sin, Death, and the human condition, we need a framework that can hold the tension of the ancient and the existential, the mythic and the embodied. What this book proposes is a tripartite monster framework: a structure of interpretation grounded in ancient Near Eastern cosmology, modern monster theory, and the theological foundations laid in my previous books (Putthoff, 2017; 2020).

This framework allows us to see how the Bible is not merely using "monsters" as colorful metaphors. Rather, it invites us to take seriously the possibility that Sin and Death are actual beings—divine-but-degenerate agents—who function in theological and anthropological roles with terrifying precision. They are not just what happens to humans. They are what takes up residence within them. The three "layers" of this framework can be understood as follows.

### Layer 1—Mythic Function: Monsters as Cosmic Actors

In the ancient world, monsters were not side characters—they were gods at war. Tiamat (Babylonian), Mōt (Ugaritic), Yamm (Canaanite), Leviathan (Israelite), and others were not abstract symbols of disorder—they were the embodiment of chaos itself. They were beings who challenged the Creator, who sought to unravel the ordered world by returning it to pre-creation sludge. In the *Baal Cycle*, Mōt swallows the life-giving god Baal, interrupting fertility and rainfall, initiating cosmic drought. In *Enuma Elish*, Tiamat births monstrous offspring who war against the young gods. These figures are not "villains" in the literary sense—they are theological threats to existence.

The Bible participates in this tradition but with its own twist. Leviathan becomes YHWH's plaything (Psalm 104:26) or sacrificial victim (Isaiah 27:1). Māwet is taunted (Hosea 13:14) and swallowed in turn (Isaiah 25:8). These creatures do not disappear—they are subjugated. The mythic battle continues, but in biblical theology, YHWH alone is victorious.

Now enter Sin and Death. In Paul's writings, these forces are not merely the results of human disobedience—they are personified and powerful entities, waging war against both God and humanity. They are cosmic saboteurs with agency, appetite, and strategy. Paul echoes the *Chaoskampf* not with dragons and sea monsters, but with invasive spirits that corrupt from within. Sin "seizes opportunity" (Romans 7:8), "deceives" and "kills" (7:11), "dwells in me" (7:17). Death "reigns" (5:14), and must be defeated (1 Corinthians 15:26).

In this function, monsters are not metaphors. They are characters in the divine drama—cosmic players whose job is to unravel creation by hijacking the creature God made as his image and in his likeness.

### Layer 2—Anthropological Function: Monsters as Internal Reality

Monsters don't just act *out there* in mythic space. They reflect what's going wrong *in here*, within the human self. In both ancient literature and modern psychology, the monstrous is a way to speak of internal fracture, distortion, and disintegration.

In the Bible, humans are hybrid creatures by design (Genesis 2:7). But hybrids are unstable. We are capable of channeling the divine, but also vulnerable to being distorted by other powers. Cain becomes a killer because he gives himself over to Sin, which "crouches at the door"

(Genesis 4:7). Pharaoh becomes a monster through his hard-hearted resistance to YHWH. Nebuchadnezzar becomes beast-like because of his pride (Daniel 4). And Paul? Paul describes a version of himself that is fractured, colonized, and unable to act according to his will (Romans 7:15–23).

Psychologically, monsters function as mirrors for the fractured self. As Beal insists, monsters are more us than other, more in us than out there, and more reflections of ourselves than of something beyond us. They reflect what we suppress or fear to admit about ourselves (Beal, 2022). Freud's notion of the uncanny—the familiar made frightening—captures this perfectly. And in Paul's letters, we find the *egō* not as sovereign, rational agent, but as a battlefield. "It is no longer I who do it, but Sin dwelling in me" (Romans 7:17). The human being, in Paul's anthropology, is monstrous not by choice, but by colonization, by invasion.

This symbolic-anthropological lens allows us to see Sin and Death as not only cosmic forces but also internal deformers. They shape identity. They override desire. They make us do what we hate—and keep us from doing what we long to do. They twist the divine likeness into something grotesque. Paul is not just writing theology here. He is drawing a profile of the haunted self.

## Layer 3—Cosmological Function: Monsters as Indwelling Powers

The final—and perhaps most unsettling—layer of the framework is this: monsters don't just symbolize disorder. They inhabit.

This is where Paul is most radical. He speaks of Sin and Death not just as enemies or influences, but as indwellers. Sin lives "in me" (Romans 7:17, 20). Death rules in my body (Romans 5:14, 17). The *sarx* ("flesh") becomes the arena, the lair, the place where divine order is resisted from within. The body is no longer a temple of God—it is a house occupied by squatters, rival forces who resist the Creator's claim.

Here, Paul is building on a worldview well attested in the ancient Near East: that gods can inhabit human bodies. I have argued elsewhere that divine embodiment was a foundational aspect of royal and prophetic identity (Putthoff, 2020). Kings, priests, and sometimes even ordinary people could become vessels of the divine. The gods acted through human bodies—granting speech, wisdom, battle strength, or prophetic sight.

But what happens when divine embodiment is hijacked? What if the beings who indwell the human are not benevolent? What if the temple has been overrun? This is precisely Paul's diagnosis. Sin and Death are not abstractions. They are divine-but-corrupt powers—fallen beings who take up residence inside the human creature and disfigure it. The very capacity that made humanity divine—its ability to be indwelt by other forces—becomes its main vulnerability. The very gift of embodiment becomes the site of catastrophe.

This is where theology, cosmology, and horror meet. The body is not just a moral playground. It is a cosmic battlefield. It is where gods and monsters clash for dominion. And every human is caught in that war.

# CHAPTER 3—DEATH AS A LIVING MONSTER

## RETHINKING DEATH IN BIBLICAL THEOLOGY

When modern readers hear the word "death," we instinctively imagine a medical event: the cessation of breath, the quiet stillness of a body, a moment marked on a certificate. Even in Christian settings, death is often framed sentimentally—as "going home," "passing on," or joining loved ones in a peaceful beyond. It is the final step in the life cycle, the natural conclusion every creature must face. But Scripture's vocabulary refuses to let death be natural, quiet, or passive. In the Hebrew Bible, *māwet* ("Death") and *še'ōl* ("Sheol") appear not only as conditions or locations but as actors—agents that pursue, swallow, bind, shepherd, and rule.

To enter the biblical world is to step into a different imaginative landscape. There, Death is not an endpoint. It is a presence. It stalks, speaks, and devours. It behaves less like a medical category and more like a monster whose appetite is never satisfied. The prophets taunt it as if it can hear (Hosea 13:14). The psalmists cry out as though it can strike (Psalm 18:4–5). Job pictures it as dwelling in tents, enthroning itself in ruined households (Job 18:13–14). This ancient vocabulary is not mere rhetorical flourish—it is ancient theology. Israel's Scriptures consistently portray Death as a force with agency—sometimes a realm, sometimes a condition, but very often a living adversary.

This is difficult terrain for contemporary readers like you and me. Centuries of philosophical influence—especially Greco-Roman dualism and later Christian scholasticism—have led to a sanitized vocabulary where death is "the natural consequence of finitude," a metaphysical boundary built into creation itself. But the Hebrew Bible does not imagine Death this way. In Israel's imagination, *mortality* may be part of creaturely existence, but Death (capital-D) is not. Mortality is the limitation of dust, while Māwet (*māwet*) is the devourer of dust. Mortality is creaturely fragility, while Sheol (*šeʾōl*) is the realm that swallows the fragile whole. Mortality speaks to what humans are. Death speaks to what threatens them.

Because of this, we must resist the temptation to collapse the biblical language of death into modern abstraction. When the psalmist says, "The cords of Death encompassed me" (Psalm 18:4), he is not claiming he nearly had a heart attack. He is describing a power that encircled him like a hunter closing a snare. When Isaiah declares that Sheol "has enlarged its appetite" (Isaiah 5:14), he is not speaking poetically about burial rates. He is describing a monster whose mouth opens wider the more it consumes. And when Hosea taunts Death—"Where are your plagues? Where is your sting?" (Hosea 13:14)—he assumes a being equipped with weapons.

In the biblical imagination, Death is not passive. It does not merely "happen" to humans. It acts upon them. Understanding this is crucial for two reasons. In the first place, it allows us to hear the Hebrew Bible on its own terms. Modern Christian discourse often treats death as theologically neutral: the "natural order of things," simply an unfortunate but expected part of life. But this is not how Israel thought. Israel feared Death not simply because it ended life, but because it assaulted life. It threatened covenant, memory, relationship, worship, and the very goodness of creation. Death was not merely "the end"—it was the undoing of God's world, the monster that unravels what God knit together.

In the second place, this framework prepares us to understand Paul. When Paul declares that "Death reigned from Adam to Moses" (Romans 5:14) or that Death is "the last enemy to be destroyed" (1 Corinthians 15:26), he is not borrowing Greek philosophical language about mortality. He is tapping into Israel's long-standing belief that Death is a tyrant—one that occupies, enslaves, and rules. Paul's vocabulary only makes sense inside the imaginative world of Isaiah, Job, the Psalms, and the mythic inheritance of Israel's neighbors.

This chapter, then, proceeds from a simple methodological conviction: to understand Death in Paul's letters and the New Testament, we must first understand Death as Israel understood it. And Israel understood it as something alive.

Before we trace the biblical texts that depict Death as a living agent, two clarifications are necessary. Firstly, the Bible speaks of "death" in more than one way. To be sure, it can refer to the moment biological life ends. It can refer to the grave. It can refer to the human condition of frailty and finitude. And it can refer to the monstrous power we are describing here. These meanings of course overlap, but they are not interchangeable. The task of the interpreter is to recognize when the text shifts from one register to another—when death is an event, and when Death is an adversary.

Secondly, this chapter focuses on Death, whereas the next chapter will mirror this work with Sin. The two powers are profoundly linked in biblical theology. Sin opens the door; Death walks through it. Sin crouches (Genesis 4:7); Death devours (Isaiah 5:14). Sin deceives and enslaves (Romans 7:11, 23); Death reigns and tyrannizes (Romans 5:14; Hebrews 2:14–15). Together, they form the twin chaos monsters behind the New Testament's language of bondage and deliverance.

To rethink biblical theology, then, we must rethink Death—not as a poetic metaphor or an existential boundary, but as Scripture presents it: a cosmic predator whose jaws, cords, snares, and throne animate the drama of creation. The importance of this ancient imagination of Death—with its appetite, its reach, its authority, and its capacity to undo creation—is that it forms the theological background to Israel's greatest hope: that YHWH will one day swallow the swallower (Isaiah 25:8) and return the world to life.

With this reframing in place, we turn now to the world of the ancient Near East—the world that influenced and gave shape to the biblical writers' ideas and conceptions of God, humanity, and the cosmos.

## DEATH IN THE ANCIENT NEAR EAST: MŌT THE DEVOURER

If Israel speaks of Death as a living, predatory force, it does not do so in a cultural vacuum. The ancient Near East already imagined Death as a deity, and the figure who most clearly shaped Israel's symbolic world was the Ugaritic god, Mōt. To read the Hebrew Bible without this background is to hear only half the conversation. Mōt is not merely a mythological artifact. He is the cultural shadow behind Israel's personified Death (*māwet*) and the ravenous domain of Sheol (*še'ōl*). He is the template that helps us understand why biblical writers instinctively reached for jaws, cords, snares, and thrones when they spoke of Death.

### Mōt as Divine Death in Ugarit

In Ugaritic myth, written in a Northwest Semitic language closely related to Hebrew, the Ugaritic word *mōt* means exactly what its Hebrew cognate *māwet* means: "death." But at Ugarit, Mōt is not a concept. He is a divine being—a god in his own right, seated within the pantheon, addressed as a person, feared as an adversary, and engaged as a force whose presence alters the world. Mōt appears most famously in the *Baal Cycle* (KTU 1.1–1.6), a collection of mythic texts centered on Baal, Anat, and the cosmic forces that sustain or threaten life.

Mōt's character is drawn with gruesome detail. His appetite is insatiable, his mouth massive, his reach unbounded. One text describes him this way. The *Baal Cycle* portrays Mōt as possessing an insatiable appetite, with a mouth stretching from earth to heaven, capable of swallowing gods and humans alike. His appetite is unending, his jaws like traps that never release. He stretches his lips to the earth's depths to devour gods and mortals alike (KTU 1.5).

Here, the language of jaws swallowing and devouring is hardly a metaphor for being buried in the ground. It is literal within the mythic world. Mōt consumes even gods—Baal included. This is not depicting the natural fading of life but a divine predator who feasts. His body is described in terms fit for a creature of horror: cavernous mouth, grasping throat, a hunger that reaches the underworld's foundations.

Israel knew these myths. Ugarit sat only a few hundred miles north of Israel; its language, religion, and imagery were part of the cultural air of the Levant. When biblical writers speak of Sheol's "open mouth" (Isaiah 5:14) or describe Death as a shepherd or ruler (Psalm 49:14; Job 18:14), they are using imagery deeply at home in the world shaped by Mōt.

## The Appetite of Mōt and the Cyclic Struggle with Baal

Mōt's most defining characteristic is not simply that he kills. It is that he consumes. He is appetite incarnate. In the *Baal Cycle*, Mōt swallows Baal—the storm god whose rains grant fertility and agricultural life. When Baal descends into Mōt's throat, creation collapses. The fields dry, the rains cease, vegetation shrivels, and even the gods mourn. The text portrays a cosmos suspended, stalled between life and decay.

But Mōt's triumph is never final. Through the intervention of Anat, Baal's sister—a goddess of extraordinary ferocity—Baal is restored. Mōt is defeated. Yet the conflict is never conclusively settled. Mōt returns season after season, echoing the agricultural cycles of drought and renewal. His victories are real but temporary, and his defeats are significant but never permanent.

This cycle mattered theologically. It taught the ancient world that life was always under threat. Death was not a static boundary at life's conclusion but an active force pressing continually into the realm of the living. To live was to resist Mōt, and to flourish was somehow to outrun him another season.

This is the world Israel inherited. This is why the biblical authors routinely speak of Death as a power that "reigns" (Romans 5:14), "rules" (Psalm 49:14), "binds" (Psalm 18:4–5), and "devours" (Isaiah 5:14). To the ancients, these are not exaggerations. They are the theological grammar of a world where Death acted like a god.

## Mōt as "Template" for Israel's Personified Death

Israel did not simply adopt Ugaritic mythology wholesale—its theology of YHWH consistently challenged, transformed, and contradicted the assumptions of its neighbors. But Israel did absorb the imagery. The picture of Death as animate, hungry, and forceful was part of the Near Eastern symbolic system.

Scholars such as John Day and Jon Levenson have demonstrated how biblical writers make selective use of this mythic vocabulary (Day, 1985; 2000; Levenson, 1988). Death (*māwet*) and Sheol (*še'ōl*) appear in Israel's Scriptures not merely as places of burial or abstract fates but as active agents with mouths, snares, cords, hands, and authority.

In fact, *māwet* in the Hebrew Bible is sometimes so personified that it functions grammatically like a proper noun—behaving like a character rather than a condition. When Hosea says, "O Death (*māwet*), where are your plagues?" (Hosea 13:14), the prophet speaks *to* Death, not *about* it. The same is true when the psalmists plead for deliverance from Death's cords or Sheol's grasp. The language presumes a being who can act, respond, or be resisted.

Mōt provides the cultural and conceptual analogue that we as modern Christians have a hard time understanding. He demonstrates how a Semitic world could speak of Death as if it were alive without collapsing into dualism or mythology. Israel's Scriptures operate within this inherited symbolic environment but press it toward a different theological horizon: YHWH, not Mōt, is the sovereign one. And Death, no matter how ravenous, is not ultimate.

## Why This Background Matters for the Biblical Portrait

Understanding Mōt clarifies why Israel's depiction of Death is so vigorous, so physical, so animate. Without this background, the Hebrew Bible might appear simply to use poetic flourish—hyperbole, exaggerated metaphor, which is how many of us tend to read such texts today. But with Mōt in view, the imagery comes into focus: Death in Israel behaves like Death in Ugarit. It swallows. It hunts, shepherds, and enthrones itself, and its appetite is never satisfied.

This does not mean Israel is borrowing mythology uncritically. It means Israel is interpreting the human condition through categories already available in its cultural world. The New Testament will later do the same when it speaks of Death as a reigning tyrant (Romans 5:14) or an enemy to be destroyed (1 Corinthians 15:26). Paul inherits not only Israel's Scripture but Israel's symbolic universe—and behind that universe stands Mōt, the archetype of Death as monster.

To grasp the personified Death of the Bible, then, we must first understand the world that taught people to imagine Death with jaws. And having set that stage, we now turn to Israel's own vocabulary to explore how the Hebrew Bible reshapes, intensifies, and reinterprets this ancient Near Eastern imagination.

## MĀWET AND SHEOL: ISRAEL'S DEATH-COMPLEX

If Ugaritic myth gives us Mōt as the archetypal death-god, Israel's Scriptures present a more intricate and layered picture. The Hebrew Bible does not preserve a single, tidy definition of Death. Instead, it operates with what we might understand as a death-complex: a constellation of terms, images, and functions clustered around two central words—*māwet* ("Death") and *šeʾōl* ("Sheol"). These two are not synonyms, but neither are they cleanly separable. They behave together, appear together, and bleed into one another in ways that resist rigid lexical boundaries. To understand how Israel imagined Death as a living agent, we must allow *māwet* and *šeʾōl* to remain slightly unstable— sometimes place, sometimes power, sometimes figure (Levenson, 1988; Day, 2000).

### Why Treat Māwet and Šeʾōl Together?

Modern interpreters often want discrete definitions: *māwet* means "death," *šeʾōl* means "grave" or "underworld." But Israel's poets and prophets do not always honor these distinctions. In many texts, *māwet* acts like a force that pursues and devours, while *šeʾōl* behaves like a creature with a mouth, appetite, or reach. At times, *māwet* functions as an agent serving the realm of *šeʾōl*. At other times, *šeʾōl* seems to be the embodiment of *māwet*. The boundaries remain fluid because the realities are fluid.

Scholars have long recognized that the Hebrew Bible's depiction of Death draws from and reshapes ancient Near Eastern mythic patterns. Levenson, for example, argues that Israel inherited an older cosmic conflict tradition—one in which divine forces of life and death battle for the cosmos—and then reframed it within Israel's monotheistic vision of YHWH's sovereignty (Levenson, 1988). Day likewise highlights how the imagery of swallowing, cords, pits, and monstrous mouths reflects an ancient mythic background, even when Israel uses those images to proclaim YHWH's superiority (Day, 1985; 2000).

In short: Israel's imagery of Death cannot be confined to one dictionary entry. It is a living symbolic network in which *māwet* and *šeʾōl* operate together to portray Death as animate, invasive, and predatory.

## Realm, Force, or Figure? The Necessary Ambiguity

Three overlapping roles emerge when we look closely at how the Hebrew Bible uses these terms. One, Death as a realm. Sometimes *šeʾōl* is geographic—the shadowy underworld, the place to which all the dead descend (e.g., Psalm 6:5; Job 7:9). It has a location ("down"), a population ("all who go down to the dust"), and an atmosphere ("darkness," "silence," "forgetfulness").

Two, Death as a force. At other moments, *māwet* functions like a cosmic force that sweeps across the earth. The destroyer (*hammašḥīt*), Death's agent, claims the firstborn (Exodus 12:23), haunts battlefields (Jeremiah 9:21), and wields plagues or famine as tools of devastation. In these scenes, *māwet* resembles Mōt—not merely the event of dying but the active force that makes dying happen.

Three, Death as a figure. Still other passages speak of *māwet* or *šeʾōl* as though they were living beings—opening mouths, stretching throats, laying snares, binding victims with cords, shepherding flocks, or reigning like kings (e.g., Isaiah 5:14; Psalm 49:14; Job 18:14). These are not metaphors for decomposition. They are actions attributed to an agent.

Rather than choosing between these roles, the Hebrew Bible holds them in productive tension. Realm, force, and figure together convey the depth of the threat. Death is not merely where humans go, nor simply what happens at the end of life. It is what hunts them, what binds them, what rules them, and what claims its own.

## A Method for Reading Death as an Agent

Because *māwet* ("death") and *šeʾōl* ("Sheol") are so multivalent, it is easy for modern readers to treat the more vivid, personifying language as mere poetic flourish. This is typically what we modern interpreters do when we encounter terms or ideas that seem too far-fetched. But when we look across the canonical texts, the consistency is striking. Death appears not as a literary device but as a recurring character.

To make this visible, the rest of the chapter proceeds in a systematic way. Rather than moving chronologically or thematically through one book at a time, we track the behaviors of Death across genres and periods. We ask: What does Death do? And whenever we find verbs, actions, or images that signal agency, appetite, hostility, or rule, we pause and examine the text closely—its vocabulary, its context, its cultural resonances.

This method allows us to see patterns that are otherwise easy to miss. When Isaiah speaks of Sheol widening its throat, when the psalmist describes Death's cords wrapping around his body, when Job calls Death the "king of terrors," these are not isolated flourishes. They are pieces of a coherent symbolic grammar. The patterns only emerge when we allow *māwet* and *še'ōl* to function together as Israel's composite portrayal of the power that undoes and devours life.

### The Significance of This Approach

By treating *māwet* and *še'ōl* as part of a unified death-complex, we take seriously the theological world of the biblical authors. We honor the imagery on its own terms rather than forcing it into modern, medicalized categories. And we prepare ourselves to see why Paul so naturally personifies Death as a tyrant in Romans 5–8: he stands within this very tradition.

Even more importantly, understanding Israel's depiction of Death as agent rather than abstraction allows us to grasp the stakes of the biblical story. If Death is a monster—hungry, cunning, relentless—then Israel's hope in YHWH is not a sentimental reassurance but a survival claim. Only a God stronger than Death can redeem Israel. Only a God who can swallow the swallower (Isaiah 25:8) can restore creation.

With this framework in hand, we now walk—systematically— through the Hebrew texts where *māwet* and *še'ōl* act as living beings. We begin with the most primal image in Israel's imagination: Death as a mouth, open and widening.

## MĀWET / SHEOL AS HUNGRY MOUTH

Perhaps the most primal and unsettling image for Death in the Hebrew Bible is that of a mouth—open, widening, insatiable. Israel does not picture Death as a silent transition but as a throat that stretches to consume entire populations. This imagery is not incidental—it is foundational. It is the place where the biblical imagination meets the older mythic grammar of the ancient Near East and reshapes it for Israel's theological world. The Ugaritic god Mōt, whose appetite was "like fire" and whose jaws reached down to the earth's foundations, supplies the cultural backdrop. But in Israel's hands, this monstrous appetite becomes even more socially charged and theologically sharp.

### Isaiah 5:14—The Expanding Appetite

Nowhere is this imagery more vivid than in Isaiah 5:14:

> Therefore, Sheol has enlarged its appetite (*hirḥîḇāh še'ōl nafshāh*) and opened its mouth without measure (*pā'arāh pîhā livlî-ḥōq*) and down go her nobility, her multitude, her uproar, and her jubilant throng.

The Hebrew here is carefully chosen for maximum force. The verb *hirḥîḇāh* ("has enlarged") does not refer to static size but to active expansion—stretching, widening, distending. *Še'ōl*, normally translated "the grave" or "the underworld," behaves here like a creature loosening its jaw to swallow more prey. The phrase *pā'arāh pîhā livlî-ḥōq* means literally "it has gaped its mouth without limit." The image is grotesque: a limitless throat, gaping wide enough to engulf not merely individuals but whole communities.

Isaiah's rhetoric is both theological and political. The context is Jerusalem's pride, injustice, and revelry (Isaiah 5:11–12). Death's appetite grows in direct proportion to the city's decadence. In other words, the devouring mouth is not an impersonal force. It responds. It reacts. It adjusts its jaws to fit whatever meal human arrogance provides. Sheol is not passively waiting for the end of life. On the contrary, it is actively consuming life as it is lived.

This is precisely the kind of fluid personification that scholars have highlighted (Levenson, 1988; Day, 1985; 2000). Death is not merely a condition but a power with a will—one that can widen its throat and take more when more is offered. It is the biblical reshaping of Mōt's appetite into a moral horizon.

### Proverbs 27:20—The Unsatisfied Maw

This same disturbing image appears in Wisdom tradition, where it is stripped down to its essential theological claim. Proverbs 27:20 declares:

> Sheol and Abaddon are never satisfied (*lō' tisba'nāh*); and human eyes are never satisfied.

The parallel is striking. *Še'ōl* is paired with *'Abaddōn*—a term referring either to the realm of destruction or a figure associated with it (cf. Job

26:6; Proverbs 15:11; Revelation 9:11). Together, they function as a double-name for Death's domain and its administrator. And the claim is absolute: they are "never satisfied." The verb *sāba'* normally refers to being filled or satisfied (Putthoff, 2017). Here, its negation highlights a bottomless appetite. Death does not grow full or reach equilibrium. It is defined by hunger.

The comparison to "human eyes" is not trivial. In Wisdom literature, the eyes represent desire—endless, roaming, insatiable (Proverbs 27:20; 30:15–16; Ecclesiastes 1:8). The proverb suggests that human desire mirrors the monstrous appetite of Death. The hunger that consumes us is, in its own way, Death working within us. The semantic field of appetite, desire, and consumption binds the two together: humans imitate the monster that devours them.

### Proverbs 1:12—Death as Swallowing Beast

Proverbs 1:12 goes further still, placing a predatory metaphor on the lips of violent men who invite the young to join their crimes:

> Let us swallow them alive like Sheol (*nibla'ēm kěšō'l ḥayyīm*),
> whole, like those who go down to the pit (*temīmīm kěyōrědē bōr*).

The simile is blunt. Violent humans imitate *še'ōl*. Their predation resembles that of the underworld. The verb *bāla'*—"to swallow"—is the same used for serpents consuming prey (cf. Exodus 7:12). *Še'ōl* is imagined as a devouring beast whose way of killing is not gentle attrition but ingestion. And the men who speak these words reveal how the monstrous logic of Death seeps into human behavior: domination, violence, and exploitation are all enacted in Death's image.

Here, we move from cosmic poetry to moral psychology. Death's appetite becomes a template for human cruelty. In Wisdom's view, one does not merely die like everyone else. One instead becomes like what kills everyone else. Death's hunger, when we feast at his table too long, eventually becomes our own.

### Habakkuk 2:5—The Enlarged Appetite of Greed

Another text, often overlooked in discussions of Death imagery, appears in Habakkuk 2:5:

> He enlarges his appetite like Sheol (*hirḥīḇ kěšō'l napšō*),
> and like Death (*kěmāwet*) he is never satisfied (*wělō' yisba'*).

Here, the prophet describes the Babylonian empire, personifying its greed and violence using the same imagery the Bible uses for Death.

Empire expands its territory the same way Death expands its throat—ceaselessly, ravenously, without limit. The parallel is intentional: the conquering nation is a living embodiment of *māwet* and *šeʾōl*. Imperial conquest is another version of the monster's mouth.

This is Israel's theological genius: the symbols are not relegated to mythic realms. They move into history. Nations act like Death because Death acts through them. The empire's hunger and the grave's hunger are the same appetite manifest in different registers. It is precisely this convergence that later biblical writers, and Paul especially, will draw upon when interpreting human and cosmic evil as intertwined.

## Mōt in the Background, Israel in the Foreground

In each of these texts, the imagery evokes Mōt's voracious appetite—the god who "opens his jaws" and "stretches out his throat" to consume gods and mortals alike. But Israel's poets and prophets do something new: they democratize the terror. Death is not merely a god at war with other deities. It is the ever-expanding maw beneath every act of injustice, violence, arrogance, or imperial conquest.

Where Ugaritic myth remains focused on Baal's seasonal struggle, Israel's prophetic and Wisdom literature brings the monstrous mouth into social and ethical space. Death consumes communities through their own corruption. It widens its throat in response to human choices. The monster is therefore not out there—it is down here, gaping at our doorsteps.

## The Semantic Field of Appetite and Agency

Across these texts we see a consistent set of verbs and images:

- *hirḥīb* ("to enlarge, expand")
- *pāʿar* ("to open wide, gape")
- *bālaʿ* ("to swallow whole")
- The negation of *sābaʿ* ("never satisfied")
- References to *napšō* ("his desire/appetite/self"), a term often associated with craving

This cluster forms a distinctive semantic field of appetite and agency. It constitutes a recognizably mythic profile—one that aligns closely with Mōt but is now adapted to Israel's monotheistic theology. Death has will, desire, capacity, and relational responsiveness. Most frighteningly, it does not merely *receive* the dead, but it *seeks* the living.

## The Mouth as the First Signal of a Monster

Throughout the ancient world, the mouth is one of the primary markers of monstrosity. From Mesopotamian dragons to Ugaritic chaos-beasts, the enlarged or insatiable mouth symbolizes a being whose nature is consumption. When the Hebrew Bible places this mouth on *še'ōl*, it is not choosing poetic fanfare. It is naming the nature of the adversary.

Death devours because devouring is what Death is.

With this image established—the gaping mouth, expanding and unsatisfied—we can now move to the next facet of the biblical death-complex: Death not only swallows its prey but hunts it.

## MĀWET / SHEOL AS HUNTER AND TRAPPER

If the open mouth of Sheol represents Death's appetite, the next set of biblical images reveals its tactics. Death does not merely swallow what lies still. It pursues what moves. It stalks, ambushes, ensnares, encircles. In these texts—especially in the Psalms—*māwet* and *še'ōl* act not as horizons but as hunters. The language shifts from ingestion to entrapment, from the image of the devouring maw to that of ropes, nets, snares, and torrents. Here, Death is not a passive end but an active force closing in on the living, employing the tools of ancient Near Eastern warfare and wild-game hunting.

This imagery also reflects Israel's lived world. In a landscape where shepherds, soldiers, and farmers regularly encountered animal traps, ambushes, flash floods in wadis, and military encirclement, the metaphor was immediate. To be ensnared was not poetic. It was a lived danger. The psalmists reach for these images because they make visceral sense. Death is not simply waiting. It is hunting.

### Psalm 18 / 2 Samuel 22—Death as Encircling Hunter

One of the most concentrated clusters of this predatory imagery appears in Psalm 18:4–5 (paralleled in 2 Samuel 22:5–6):

> The cords of Death encompassed me (*'ăfāfunī ḥevlē māwet*);
> the torrents of Belial terrified me (*venaḥălē beliyya'al yeba'ătūnī*);
> the cords of Sheol surrounded me (*ḥevlē še'ōl sevāvūnī*);
> the snares of Death confronted me (*qiddĕmūnī moqshē māwet*).

Every phrase is designed to constrict the reader.

The verb *'āfaf* ("encircled, enveloped") evokes the tightening of ropes around the body. The noun *ḥevel* ("cord, rope") is used elsewhere for boundary lines (Joshua 17:5), indicating both confinement and claim of territory. In this context, the cord is a hunting tool, as Death is binding and enclosing its target. The parallelism with *moqshē māwet* ("snares of Death") confirms the predatory nature of this imagery. The *moqesh*—a trap—was often a hidden device that would snap shut or entangle when stepped on, frequently used for birds or small animals.

In the ancient Near East, nets and snares were everywhere—used for hunting, capturing enemies, even symbolic of judicial punishment. To the psalmist, being "surrounded" by Death's cords is to feel the sudden, immobilizing fear of prey caught in a trap. It is not gradual aging but sudden ambush.

The "torrents of Belial" intensify the sense of the suddenness of attack. Seasonal wadis in Judea could appear safe until a cloudburst miles upstream sent a wall of water surging through the valley—this is still a dangerous phenomenon today. Many would have died in swift, unexpected floods. That is what the psalmist compares Death to: not a slow decline but a sudden, violent engulfing. The association of *beliyya'al* with chaotic forces (cf. Nahum 1:11; 2 Corinthians 6:15) underscores that Death hunts with the unpredictability of a flash flood.

Here, *māwet* and *še'ōl* behave like coordinated hunters—setting traps, tightening cords, and driving the prey toward the final kill.

### Psalm 116:3—The Grasping Hands of Death

Psalm 116:3 revisits and intensifies the imagery:

> The cords of Death encircled me (*'ăfāfūnī ḥevlē māwet*);
> the pangs of Sheol found me (*ūmĕṣarē še'ōl metsā'ūnī*);
> I found distress and sorrow.

The phrase *mĕṣarē še'ōl* ("the pangs/bindings of Sheol") is particularly evocative. The term *mēṣar* can refer to narrowness or constriction, as in a tight, deathlike grip. Interestingly, the term also appears in contexts of birth pangs (e.g., Jeremiah 4:31), suggesting a dark reversal: instead of a mother laboring to bring forth the life of creation, Sheol labors to pull life back into the womb of uncreation. It is a grotesque inversion—birth pangs that do not deliver but devour.

The verb *māṣā'* ("found, seized") adds another layer of menace. The pangs of Sheol do not merely exist. They instead search, locate, and apprehend. Death is on the move, not waiting idly for time to claim its due.

The psalmist's response—"I found distress and sorrow"—is not only emotional despair but recognition of being hunted. The language mirrors that of fugitives fleeing captors (Psalms 18:4–5; 116:3; 142:3–

4). Death here is not an abstract transition at the end of life. It is a pursuer with hands.

### Proverbs 5:22—The Self as Prey of Its Own Actions

Proverbs 5:22 deepens the hunter imagery by merging it with the moral sphere. It's similar to Psalm 49:14, which describes the wicked being shepherded to Sheol, and which we will explore more in the next section. The Proverb, however, associates misdeeds with entrapment:

> Their own iniquities shall capture the wicked (*avonotav yilkĕdūnō*); they are held fast in the cords of their Sin (*beḥavlē ḥaṭṭā'tō yitāmāk*, Proverbs 5:22).

Though this text speaks technically of Sin rather than Death, the imagery is the same: cords, capture, snares. The semantic field is identical because the conceptual field is continuous. The chaos forces that ensnare the human—Sin, Death, and Sheol—share a vocabulary because they share a profile. The Psalm and Proverb traditions recognize a single monstrous ecosystem: Sin leads to sin, sins become cords, cords become traps, and traps deliver the prey into the jaws of Sheol.

This convergence is precisely what Paul will later articulate explicitly. For now, it is enough to observe that the hunter imagery is not confined to psalms of distress. It permeates Israel's moral imagination. To sin is to step willingly into the snares of Death and Sin.

### The Cultural Register of Traps and Nets

To appreciate this imagery, we must remember where these writers lived. The Judean wilderness was full of natural hazards and hunting devices. Hunters used pits covered with brush, nets strung across animal paths, bird traps triggered by slight movements, and cords designed to tighten as the prey struggled. Soldiers used similar tools in warfare, including ambush tactics, encirclement maneuvers, and flanking movements designed to cut off escape.

In this cultural environment, the imagery of being surrounded, ensnared, or overtaken was not allegorical. It was existential. The psalmist is not philosophizing; he is describing Death in terms culturally associated with actual life-threatening situations.

This is one reason the metaphors resonate so deeply. They describe Death not as a gentle transition but as a violent breach of the world's order. Death is a chaos-force seeking to disrupt the order and balance of God's good creation. Just as a hunter disrupts the calm of a field with a sudden snap of a trap, Death intrudes upon the life of the living with coercive force.

## Sheol's Strategy: Constriction, Immobilization, Capture

Across these texts a coherent strategy emerges. Death hunts in three movements:

1. Encirclement—cords of Death (*ḥevlē māwet*) tighten like cords around the body.
2. Immobilization—snares (*moqshīm*) confront and disable.
3. Capture—the prey is "found" by the pangs of Sheol and carried off.

This sequence is not invented whole cloth by any single psalmist. It is instead a theological grammar shared across Israel's Wisdom texts and hymns. Death is not merely where one ends up. It is what stalks one along the way.

## A Theological Point Hidden in a Hunter's Image

What is most striking is the psalmists' refusal to accept Death's pursuit as a neutral or inevitable feature of existence. The cry for deliverance arises because Death's hunt is illegitimate. YHWH alone is rightful shepherd, rightful king, rightful judge. Death is a usurper. It takes what is not its own.

This is why the psalmists cry out with urgency—not because Death's cords are part of the natural order, but because they violate the natural order. They are an intrusion, an attack, a monstrous breach. To appeal to YHWH is to appeal to the one who can cut cords (Psalm 129:4), break snares (Psalm 124:7), and rescue prey from the hunter's trap (Psalm 91:3).

Death's cords are strong. But they are cuttable.

## DEATH AS SHEPHERD, KING, AND RULER

If the hungry mouth and hunting snare portray Death as predator, the next set of biblical images shifts to a different kind of horror—one rooted not in sudden attack but in sovereignty. In these texts, *māwet* is not simply a devourer or ambusher but a ruler. He carries titles, exercises authority, inhabits dwellings, marshals weapons, and shepherds populations. The metaphors draw from political life: shepherds who guide flocks, kings who rule their territories, warlords who terrorize subjects, and invaders who occupy homes. When Israel's writers describe Death in these terms, they are not speaking loosely.

They are framing *māwet* as a rival sovereign whose rule stands in direct competition with YHWH's.

This political imagery is crucial because it reveals how Israel understood the problem of Death. Mortality is not merely a biological fact to be accepted. It is a kingdom to be overthrown. To speak of Death as king is to name a regime. To speak of Death as shepherd is to name a rival leadership. To speak of Death as armed is to name an enemy in battle. In each case, the language of authority is used deliberately to signal that Death's power is real, invasive, and illegitimate.

### Psalm 49:14—Death as Shepherd

The most startling royal metaphor appears in Psalm 49:14:

> Like sheep they are appointed for Sheol (*kaṣṣōn lišʾōl šattu*); Death shall be their shepherd (*māwet yirʿēm*). And the upright shall rule over them in the morning.

This reversal of Psalm 23 is not incidental. Israel's most beloved psalm pictures YHWH as shepherd (*raʿah*), leading the psalmist through "the valley of the shadow of Death" (*gēʾ ṣalmāwet*) and out again into security. But in Psalm 49, the shepherd is *māwet* himself. Death holds the staff. Death guides the flock. Death is the one whose voice the sheep follow.

The Hebrew *māwet yirʿēm* is emphatic—Death is performing the active role of shepherding. The verb *raʿah* in shepherding contexts involves governance: providing direction or determining movement, granting or withholding sustenance, protecting or exposing. Shepherds are rulers in pastoral miniature. Thus, to place Death in this role is to portray him as one who orders the movement of the wicked, corralling them toward their destination as surely as YHWH guides the righteous toward theirs.

The opening line reinforces the point: the wicked are "appointed" (*šattu*) for Sheol. The term carries the sense of designation or assignment. This is not the randomness of mortality but the patterned movement of a flock under a shepherd's control. Death is not gathering spontaneously; he is directing. He possesses the flock, and the flock is following.

The psalm's contrast between "morning" and the current night of Death's rule anticipates resurrection hope in a time when "the upright shall rule over them in the morning," but that eschatological reversal only makes sense if Death's rule is understood as real and active. This is not metaphorizing. It is political theology in which the world lies under rival shepherds.

### Job 18:13–14—Death as King of Terrors

If the shepherd is the ruler of the open field, the king is the ruler of the household—and Job 18 presents Death occupying both:

> It devours parts of his skin (*yō'khal baddē 'ōrō*). Death's firstborn devours his limbs. He is torn from the security of his tent and brought before the king of terrors (*melekh ballāhōt*, Job 18:13–14).

This passage gives us one of the most formal titles assigned to Death in the Hebrew Bible: *melekh ballāhōt*—"king of terrors." The plural *ballāhōt* ("terrors") underscores not only the king's demeanor but his domain. He presides over terror. He governs it. His rule is characterized by fear, disintegration, and the collapse of order.

The royal imagery is layered. First, Death devours flesh, a grotesque echo of Mōt in the *Baal Cycle*, who gruesomely eats gods and mortals indiscriminately. Second, Death evicts the victim from his tent—a breach of domestic security. In the ancient world, one's tent or house was not just shelter, but it was identity, inheritance, stability. To be "torn" (*yinnāteq*) from the tent implies violent dispossession. Death here behaves like an invading sovereign, displacing inhabitants and claiming their dwelling as his own.

Then comes the final humiliation: the victim is marched "before the king of terrors," as one brought in chains to a conqueror's throne. The image is juridical and political. Death is not simply a force or stage at the end of life. He is a monarch who holds court.

This royal depiction explains why Paul's later language of Death "reigning" (*ebasileusen*, Romans 5:14, 17) is not some metaphorical innovation. It is inherited. Job has already shown us Death enthroned—and enthralling.

### Hosea 13:14—Death as Warrior Armed for Battle

In Hosea 13:14, we find a different facet of Death's sovereignty—not domestic or pastoral or judicial, but militaristic:

> O Death, where are your plagues (*'ehī devarēkha māwet*)?
> O Sheol, where is your sting (*'ehī qaṭāvekhā še'ōl*)?

This taunt only works because Death and Sheol are envisioned as armed enemies. The nouns *dever* ("plague") and *qaṭav* ("sting, poison") evoke the arsenal of divine judgment—disease, pestilence, venom. These were not abstract symbols in antiquity like we think of them. For the ancients, they were weapons. The gods of the ancient Near East often wielded plague as a tool of warfare, like YHWH against Pharaoh's Egypt or the Mesopotamian deity Erra against her enemies. Death shares the same toolkit, the same weaponry.

Hosea's rhetorical question—"Where are your plagues? Where is your sting?"—is a prophetic mockery, a stripping of weapons. The implication is that Death normally possesses them. He is expected to attack with these instruments, to strike, to wound, to poison. Hosea announces a moment, however, when Death's armory is emptied.

The verse later becomes foundational for Paul's resurrection taunt in 1 Corinthians 15:54–55. But Paul's Christological appropriation works only because Hosea has already framed Death as a warrior whose defeat can be announced in the language of disarmament.

### Death's Sovereignty in Context: Not Fiction but Framework

Across these texts—Psalms, Wisdom, prophecy—a consistent portrait emerges. Death is not merely a fate. Death is a ruler. He occupies social roles typically reserved for human and divine authority figures. He guides like a shepherd, judges like a king, invades like a warlord, and disciplines like a plague-god.

This is not incidental language. It represents a worldview in which Death exerts real authority within the cosmos, an authority that must be recognized before it can be resisted. This was the world of the biblical writers.

Two implications follow. One, Death's rule is illegitimate. In the Hebrew Bible, only YHWH is rightful shepherd (Psalm 23), rightful king (Psalm 93), rightful warrior (Exodus 15). When Death occupies these roles, it is usurpation. Death is not part of the created order's intended hierarchy. He is a rogue sovereign, one who rules because humanity has fallen under his power (cf. Genesis 3; Romans 5).

Two, Death's rule is political, not merely personal. The metaphor is not private despair but public proclamation. To call Death "king" is to perceive a cosmic regime—an empire of dissolution that structures human existence. It controls destiny, speaks with authority, and enforces its rule. Israel's writers are describing not only what death is but what it does to the world.

This political dimension sets the stage for the New Testament's proclamation of Jesus' resurrection as a regime change. Christ is not merely overcoming personal mortality. He is overthrowing a kingdom.

By portraying Death with shepherd's staff, royal crown, and warrior's weapons, the Hebrew Bible declares that the enemy is not merely an impersonal process but a sovereign power. Death rules, but his rule is temporal. His weapons are sharp, but they will one day fail. His shepherding gathers flocks, but another shepherd is coming. His throne terrifies, but another throne is greater.

Israel's hope is not that Death will become kinder. It is that Death will be dethroned.

## DEATH AS UNCREATION AND ANTI-CREATION

Up to this point, the biblical texts we have examined depict Death as predator, shepherd, king, warlord—roles that presuppose a world already formed and functioning. But several passages push past these metaphors into something even more primal. Here, Death is not just a ruler within creation; it is the unraveling of creation itself. In these texts, *māwet* and *šeʾōl* are portrayed not simply as endpoints but as forces of uncreation, agents that reverse the ordering acts of Genesis 1 and drag the world back toward the primal disorder—*tōhū wābōhū* ("formless and void")—from which it was made.

This is one of the most profound theological moves in the Hebrew Bible. Death is not only the cessation of life. It is the collapse of God's creative work. It is anti-Genesis, the undoing of ordered reality. If Genesis 1 depicts creation as God conquering chaos, pushing back darkness, separating waters, establishing boundaries, introducing *sēder* ("order") where there was none, then the realm of Death represents those boundaries eroded, those separations collapsed, the light swallowed into darkness and the resurrection of chaos once again.

### Job 10:21–22—The Geography of Uncreation

Few texts express this reversal of creation as sharply as Job 10:21–22. In his lament, Job describes the realm toward which he feels himself descending:

> A land of deep darkness (*ʿerets ʿēfātāh kemo-ʾophel*),
> of gloom without order (*ṣalmāwet wĕloʾ sĕdarim*),
> where light is like darkness (*wattōfaʿ kemo-ʾophel*).

Every line here is crafted from the vocabulary of Genesis—but inverted. Creation begins with God speaking light into darkness (Genesis 1:3). Job imagines a place where light itself has collapsed, where "light is like darkness," as if the categories upon which creation depends have been

45

scrambled. Hebrew uses *ṣalmāwet* ("deep darkness," "shadow of death") rather than *ḥōshek* (ordinary "darkness"), suggesting an intensified, oppressive gloom—the kind often associated with dying prematurely.

The reference to "no order" (*lō' sĕdārīm*) is even more striking. In Genesis, creation proceeds precisely through acts of ordering, not just by bringing things into being from nothing. The cosmos come into being when God first brings order out of disorder and proceeds to separate light from darkness, waters above from waters below, land from sea. In Job's vision, the structures that sustain life are undone. The phrase suggests not merely chaos but disintegration—creation's architecture collapsing in on itself.

Several rabbinic texts later pick up this theme. In b. *Soṭah* 49a, the sages lament an age when the order (*sēder*) of the world is overturned, and there is no day without a curse (Putthoff, 2017). Job's language anticipates this—Death is the place where the world's God-given order is reversed. It is not merely the end of a life. It is the complete undoing of creation.

### Psalm 88—Where Praise Cannot Rise

Psalm 88 intensifies the same idea through the absence of something central to Israel's understanding of life: praise. In verses 10–12, the psalmist asks:

> Do you work wonders (*pĕle'īm*) for the dead?
> Do the shades (*rephā'īm*) rise up to praise you?
> Is your steadfast love (*ḥesed*) declared in the grave,
> or your faithfulness (*'ĕmūnāh*) in Abaddon?
> Are your wonders (*pĕle'īm*) known in the darkness
> or your righteousness in the land of forgetfulness? (v. 12)

The implied answer to each question is an emphatic "no." The logic is simple: creation exists so that God's life-giving character—"steadfast love" (*ḥesed*), "faithfulness" (*'ĕmūnah*), "wonders" (*pĕle'īm*)—may be enacted and witnessed. In the realm of Death, those realities cannot be enacted. The place of Death is a theological vacuum, a space where the Creator's fundamental attributes do not function.

Psalm 88 does not deny God's sovereignty. Rather, it describes the horizon of created life. Death is not simply the end of biological breath. It is a counter-realm where God's creative purposes are suspended. The psalmist is not asking abstract questions about afterlife metaphysics the way we might do today. He is lamenting the intrusion of anti-creation into his experience of the world.

This makes the psalm's bleakness existential on a cosmic level. The terror is both the individual loss of sensation and consciousness and the collapse of the collective relational ecosystem in which praise, covenant, and divine presence operate.

### Ecclesiastes 9:10—The End of Human Vocation

A similar conceptual framework appears in Ecclesiastes 9:10:

> There is no work or thought or knowledge or wisdom in Sheol, to which you are going (*'ēn ma'ăseh wĕḥešbōn wĕda'at wĕḥokmā biš'ōl 'ăšer 'attā hōlēk šāmmā*).

The author of Ecclesiastes is not offering a metaphysical treatise so much as a phenomenological one. In Sheol, the fundamental activities that define human participation in creation, such as labor, wisdom, discernment, learning, all cease. Humans, in the biblical imagination, are active partners in God's ordering of the world (Genesis 2:15; Proverbs 8). When these activities stop, creation is no longer being enacted or maintained. Death here is the cessation of our creaturely role in sustaining the world that God made. Thus, in Ecclesiastes, the tragedy of Sheol is not torment, pain, or darkness, but negation, non-participation, and disconnection from the creative processes that give life meaning.

### Isaiah 25:8—God as the One Who Uncreates Uncreation

Against this oppressive vision of Death as anti-creator, Isaiah 25:8 offers a stunning reversal:

> He will swallow up Death forever (*billa' ha-māwet lāneṣaḥ*).

Here, the devourer becomes the devoured. The monster that swallowed everything is itself swallowed. Isaiah uses the very imagery that elsewhere characterizes *māwet*—the open mouth, the act of consumption—and applies it to God. In a sense, God performs an act of counter-uncreation: He uncreates the power that uncreates the world.

This is not just poetry or metaphor. The Hebrew Bible consistently frames God's saving work in terms of conflict with chaos and Death (Levenson, 1988). Here, that conflict reaches its apex. The defeat of Death is equivalent to the triumph of creation. If Death represents the collapse of structure, meaning, and vitality, then God's act of swallowing Death is the restoration of order, relationship, and life.

Isaiah 25 stands not at the end of biblical theology but at its pivot. By reversing Death's power to devour, God's work is more than the rescue of individual souls. It is how he takes back and secures the stability of creation itself. Salvation is cosmic, not merely personal.

### Death's Anti-Creation as Paul's Background

Later biblical writers, especially Paul, stand in this tradition. When he writes that "Death spread to all humanity" (Romans 5:12), he is not describing a biological inevitability but a cosmic contagion. When he calls Death "the last enemy" (1 Corinthians 15:26), he echoes the royal imagery of Job but infuses it with Isaiah's hope that this enemy will be destroyed. And when he taunts Death with Hosea's mockery—"Where, O Death, is your sting?" (1 Corinthians 15:55)—he is announcing the reversal of the reversal, the moment when uncreation is itself undone.

Paul's language of new creation (*kainē ktisis*) fits here as well (2 Corinthians 5:17). A new creation is only necessary if the old creation is under assault—not merely by human error, but by Death itself as anti-creator.

### Uncreation as the Deepest Threat

When the biblical writers portray Death as darkness, disorder, silence, and negation, they are pointing to something deeper than the end of lifespan. They are diagnosing Death as the unraveling of the world that God made. Death is the great anti-creation, the power that rolls back God's ordering acts, that erases distinctions, collapses categories, and pulls life toward the shadowy void that precedes and opposes God's creative word.

To understand Death this way is to see why its defeat must be dramatic, divine, and total. One cannot negotiate with anti-creation. One cannot domesticate it or make it meaningful. If God is to be Creator, then Death must be unmade. And this is precisely the hope Israel begins to voice—a hope that finds its most forceful expression in resurrection, where God pulls life from the clutches of uncreation and restores the world to the order it was always meant to bear.

## YHWH OVER DEATH, AND THE BIRTH OF RESURRECTION HOPE

Up to this point, the Hebrew Bible's portrayal of Death would not have surprised Israel's neighbors. Ugaritic, Mesopotamian, and Egyptian traditions likewise imagined Death as animate, hungry, and sovereign. But what Israel does next—how it reframes this shared mythic inheritance—is something far more radical. Israel recognizes Death's agency, acknowledges its power, names its appetite and sovereignty with unflinching realism, but refuses to grant it the final word.

This refusal is theological, not psychological. It emerges from Israel's foundational confession that YHWH alone is God. And if YHWH alone is God, then Death—however ravenous, however royal, however ancient—cannot ultimately reign. Israel's most daring move, then, is not to deny Death's monstrosity but to declare that YHWH can and will unmake it.

## YHWH as the One Who "Swallows the Swallower"

The clearest articulation of this eschatological conviction appears in Isaiah 25:8, which we discussed above. Here, Isaiah declares that YHWH "will swallow up Death forever (*billaʿ ha-māwet lāneṣaḥ*), and the Lord GOD will wipe away tears from all faces." The ancient metaphor is deliberately inverted. Everywhere else in Israel's Scriptures, Death is the devourer—stretching its desire (Isaiah 5:14), enlarging its appetite (Proverbs 27:20), consuming flesh (Job 18:13). But Isaiah announces a moment when Death itself will be swallowed. The predator becomes prey. The eater becomes the eaten.

This reversal is a direct theological critique of the Canaanite story of Mōt (Day, 2000). In the *Baal Cycle*, Mōt can swallow Baal, but Baal cannot destroy Mōt. At best, he can temporarily restrain him. For Isaiah, YHWH does what Baal could not do—he destroys Death, not merely delays it. Nor is this a metaphor for the acceptance of mortality. It is depicted as a cosmic act of war (Levenson, 1988). It is God's final victory over the powers that undo creation.

This is a move toward resurrection ideals because it de-naturalizes the experience of dying and places it squarely in a cosmic frame. Death is not accepted as a natural moment at the end of life, nor is it tamed or explained away. It is consumed, defeated, and its reign of terror now rests in the belly of the God of life.

## Theological Shift: Not God vs Mortality, but God vs Death

This distinction is crucial. Much later theology frames the human predicament as mortality—hence the idea that we die because we are finite creatures. But Israel's poets and prophets rarely speak this way. The problem is not finiteness but the rule of a hostile power. Mortality is not an ontological flaw but a symptom of occupation. Death reigns, therefore humans die.

This is why the defeat of Death is always framed as God's act, not as a philosophical lesson about acceptance. When YHWH "swallows up

Death," he is not comforting Israel with platitudes about life's fragility. He is overthrowing a regime. He is performing a judicial act against an illegitimate sovereign. In Israel's imagination, God does not reconcile humanity to Death—he rebels against it.

### Resurrection as Israel's Most Audacious Theological Development

Because Death is framed as a cosmic agent, the only adequate response is cosmic action. And this is where the doctrine of resurrection enters Israel's story—not as speculation about the afterlife, but as the logical conclusion of YHWH's longstanding battle against and final victory over Death. Note several particularly striking shifts toward this idea in the prophetic texts.

We see this in Isaiah's resurrection vision (Isaiah 26:19). As we read, "Your dead shall live; their bodies shall rise. You who dwell in the dust, awake and sing for joy." Far from being a note about spiritual survival or disembodied bliss, this is reversal, when Death's captives being reclaimed. Dust, which is otherwise the domain of Death, gives birth, not decay.

We also see this in Ezekiel's valley of dry bones (Ezekiel 37:1–14). Here, Ezekiel's vision is not simply national restoration but resurrection imagery. Bones reassemble, sinews stretch, flesh covers, and breath (*rūaḥ*) enters. Ezekiel imagines YHWH literally rebuilding what Death has dismantled. This is uncreation being re-created.

This is also evident in Daniel's prophetic words, when he writes, "Many who sleep in the dust of the earth shall awake" (Daniel 12:2). Here, resurrection is explicitly eschatological, and it's tied not to historical restoration but to God's final judgment. Death's rule will end. Those who lie under its power will be summoned out of it. Daniel offers a worldview in which history has a terminus, and that terminus is not decay but victory and liberation.

Across these texts, resurrection is not described in the soft, comforting language sometimes used today. It is not "moving on." It is not "rest." It is divine revolt, a rebellion. Resurrection is the jailbreak from Sheol. It is the moment when the cords of Death snap, the shepherd loses his flock, and the king of terrors is dethroned.

Paul later captures this with perfect theological succinctness, when he writes, "Death has been swallowed up in victory" (1 Corinthians 15:54). He is paraphrasing Isaiah because Isaiah laid the foundation. But even Isaiah was tapping into a much more ancient mythological framework in imagining Death as a devouring entity finally being devoured by God himself. Paul's Christological claim—that Christ's resurrection is the turning point of history—only makes sense against this older backdrop.

The early Christians did not invent resurrection to explain Jesus' empty tomb. They inherited a much older worldview that expected God to defeat Death. Jesus' resurrection was read as the moment when that expectation began to be fulfilled.

### God's Victory Over Death as the Anchor of Christian Theology

When modern Christians speak of "eternal life," they often envision spiritual immortality. But the biblical story aims at something stranger and more concrete: the destruction of Death itself. Eternal life is not a disembodied state but the result of Death's defeat.

In this frame, salvation is neither the escape from creation nor the reconciliation to mortality. It is participation in God's victory over the cosmic forces that unmake creation. And this is why the New Testament speaks the way it does—why Paul treats Death as a tyrant, why Hebrews speaks of liberation from "slavery through fear of Death" (Hebrews 2:14–15), and why Revelation pictures the final judgment as Death and Hades thrown into the lake of fire (Revelation 20:14).

The end of the Bible is not souls ascending. According to Scripture, it is Death descending into destruction. Israel's distinctive theological move was to refuse to normalize Death, to refuse to grant it moral or metaphysical legitimacy, and to imagine a world in which the Creator must—and will—destroy it. This move will shape everything that follows in the biblical story.

## SUMMARY: DEATH AS THE BIBLE'S MONSTER-IN-CHIEF

When we read the Hebrew Bible systematically, a unified portrait of this mysterious entity emerges. Death is not passive, not neutral, and not a serene boundary marking the end of life's journey. It is a living agent—predatory, royal, deceitful, and violent.

According to the biblical tradition, Death consumes with an ever-widening mouth (Isaiah 5:14; Proverbs 27:20). Death hunts and traps with cords and snares (Psalm 18; Psalm 116). Death shepherds, guiding victims like flocks (Psalm 49:14). Death rules enthroned as "king of terrors" (Job 18:14). Death arms itself, wielding plagues and poison (Hosea 13:14). Death uncreates, dragging creation back toward primordial chaos (Job 10:21–22; Psalm 88).

Taken together, these images reveal that the Bible treats Death not as a natural process but as a cosmic adversary—a monster whose character and actions parallel (and often echo) the older figure of Mōt, yet whose challenge to Israel is met with a far more decisive divine response.

This chapter has shown why the biblical writers speak this way. They are naming a power that must be defeated, not explained away. They are preparing the ground for Israel's boldest theological claim: that YHWH will swallow the swallower, overthrow the shepherd of decay, and unmake the unmaker.

And in doing so, they set the stage for the next step in the story.

For if Death behaves as a living force that binds, deceives, rules, and indwells, then Sin—its counterpart in Israel's theology—must be examined in the same light. What Death is to the body, Sin is to the self. Both are invaders. Both distort and destroy. Both require deliverance, not mere instruction.

The next chapter turns to that parallel figure. As we will see, Sin is not only something we do. It is someone we meet.

# CHAPTER 4—SIN AS A LIVING MONSTER

## RETHINKING SIN IN BIBLICAL THEOLOGY

Few words in theology carry as much accumulated baggage as "sin." For most modern readers—inside and outside the church—the word immediately evokes morality: mistakes, rules broken, bad habits, guilt. Sin is imagined primarily as disobedience, a kind of moral misstep that leaves an entry on a divine ledger. When someone says, "I sinned," the instinct is to imagine a lapse in judgment or a failure of willpower. This way of speaking has become so normalized that it can be difficult to imagine alternatives. Yet this individualistic, moralistic framework is markedly different from the one that shaped the biblical writers.

For the ancient world of the Bible, Sin was not simply the wrong thing one did. Sin was something that happened to a person, something that attached, accumulated, spread, and ruled. It was a burden that weighed the body down, a contaminant that saturated holy space, a snare that tightened around the limbs. More disturbingly, it was an invader—a force that entered the human frame and seized control. Israel's Scriptures portray Sin less as a list of infractions and more as a hostile power. Its logic is less courtroom and more battlefield.

This becomes clearer when we place Sin alongside Death. As we just saw, in the biblical imagination, Death is the external predator—the devouring mouth that stands at the edges of creation, swallowing individuals, families, and nations. Death is the monster that comes for the body. Sin, by contrast, is the monster that comes for the self. If Death is the wolf at the gate, Sin is the thing already in the house, crouched in the corner, waiting for the moment to strike. One pursues from without, while the other infiltrates from within.

This distinction matters because modern readers often flatten these categories into psychological metaphors. We read Death as a natural event, and Sin as a moral category, then assume the biblical writers must have meant the same. But they did not. When Psalmists cry that their iniquities "overwhelm" them, or that the "cords of Sin" entangle, this is not quaint poetry. It is phenomenology. It is an attempt to describe an experience of agency—not human agency, but its opposite. Likewise, when the prophets speak of Sin inscribing itself upon the heart or blinding the eyes, they are not waxing metaphorical. They are naming a real power that distorts perception and reshapes desire.

If the previous chapter argued that Death is a living monster—a power with appetite, sovereignty, and agency—this chapter makes the case that Sin stands beside it as a complementary force, but with a different mode of attack. Whereas Death consumes, Sin corrodes. Whereas Death devours from without, Sin colonizes from within. Together they form a monstrous dyad that the New Testament writers treat not as abstractions but as hostile rulers of the old creation (Romans 5–8; Hebrews 2:14–15; 1 Corinthians 15:24–28).

To rethink Sin, therefore, we must first step outside the moralistic categories that dominate contemporary discourse and step back into the world of the ancient Near East and the Hebrew Bible. In that world, Sin was not merely wrong action but cosmic misalignment, not merely infraction but contamination, and not merely choice but captivity. Sin was a burden one bore, a pollutant that clung, an entity that dwelt, a hunter that pursued, and an invader that took up residence where it did not belong.

This helps explain why biblical writers speak the way they do. Their language is not exaggerated spirituality. It reflects a cosmos in which divine and quasi-divine forces interact with human bodies and communities in tangible ways. Divine presence sanctifies, divine abandonment destroys, and rival powers invade. And human beings—hybrid creatures made of dust and divine breath—are uniquely susceptible to occupation. In such a world, Sin is not merely a human problem. It is a cosmic one.

Reframing Sin this way also clarifies why the biblical story insists that Sin must be overthrown, not merely "forgiven" in a moral, legal courtroom sense (Romans 6:14; 8:2–3). Forgiveness removes guilt, while liberation removes a tyrant. If Sin is a monster with its own agency, then human willpower is not enough. The biblical drama requires a stronger power to displace the invader and reclaim the human self as God's dwelling.

This chapter therefore approaches Sin in two intertwined ways:

1. Sin as event—something humans do—written as lowercase-S.
2. Sin as agent—something that acts upon and within humans—written as capital-S.

These two dimensions cannot be separated. In Scripture, the act is often the manifestation of a deeper presence. The wrong action is the symptom, while the occupying force is the disease. To treat sin merely as behavior is to treat a fever without reckoning with the infection that causes it.

The sections that follow trace this pattern across the ancient Near East and the Hebrew Bible. We will see how the language of Sin overlaps with that of cosmic contagion, pollution, enchanted burden, predation, blindness, and possession. And in doing so, we will begin to see why Paul speaks of Sin as a power that "dwells" in the self (Romans 7:17, 20), why Jesus treats forgiveness as liberation, and why the New Testament consistently frames salvation as an eviction and healing before it is a pardon.

Sin, in other words, is not simply what humans *do*. It is what *does* to humans. And until we recover this older grammar—this monster-grammar—we cannot understand why the biblical writers speak of Sin with such urgency, or why the Christian story insists on a deliverer stronger than the forces that occupy the human heart.

The ancient world knew what we have largely forgotten: Sin is not just an error. It is an entity. And the battle against it begins not with better choices, but with the recognition that the foe is alive.

## SIN IN THE ANCIENT NEAR EAST: COSMIC POLLUTANT AND DEMONIC BURDEN

To understand what Israel and later Paul mean when they speak of Sin, we have to widen our lens beyond modern categories and reenter the symbolic world of the ancient Near East. In that world, "sin" was not merely a violation of moral expectation. It was a rupture in the fabric of reality—a tear in the cosmic order that produced tangible, dangerous consequences. The Mesopotamian imagination consistently viewed sin not primarily as a legal infraction but as a force, a weight, and a contamination. It belonged far more to the realm of ritual purity, cosmic maintenance, and spiritual danger than to the realm of private morality.

### Sin as Misalignment with the Divine Order

In Akkadian texts, terms like *ḫaṭṭu* and *arnu* describe wrongdoing, but their semantic field extends well beyond what modern readers associate with ethics. These words often imply "misalignment" or "offense" against the cosmic structure. To sin is to fall out of harmony with the rhythm of the divine world—to disturb the equilibrium between gods, land, and people. In that sense, sin is something like cosmic noise or pollution. It disrupts the fragile balance that allows the gods to bless the land and its inhabitants.

This explains why so many Mesopotamian rituals focus not on remorse, but on removal. The primary problem with sin is not guilt, but presence. Sin sticks. It clings. It behaves less like a moral misstep and more like a contaminant that must be purged.

Sin, in other words, is a chaos-maker. It wrecks the order of the cosmos that the creator gods or God went to great lengths to establish. It is thus not about personal morality—it's about the continuation of the order of the cosmos. If it is allowed to remain or continue, it has the potential to thrust the entire universe into utter disorder.

### Sin as Accumulated Burden in The Šurpu Series

One of the clearest examples comes from the *Šurpu* series, an Akkadian incantation ritual used for the fiery cleansing from accumulated wrongs (Simons, 2017). The speaker confesses an exhaustive list of possible sins—acts done knowingly or unknowingly, individually or inherited. However, the issue is not whether the wrong was intentional but whether its residue remains. Sin is a burden that weighs the person down, a kind of spiritual heaviness that threatens life. The solution is transference to an object, then burning or dissolving (*Šurpu* II). The verbs emphasize destruction of a substance, not forgiveness of a deed.

Rituals like these and the *Maqlū* text treat sin as a sort of oppressive weight that attaches to the body and that must be violently removed (Abusch, 2015). The concern is not moral remorse but metaphysical hygiene.

### Sin as Quasi-Autonomous Pollutant in The Maqlū Series

The *Maqlū* (Akkadian for "burning") texts sharpen this picture even further. *Maqlū* (primarily an anti-witchcraft ritual) assumes that harm behaves like an invasive presence that must be identified, confronted, and driven out through ritual action. It suggests that evil is a dangerous presence to be removed rather than merely regretted (*Maqlū* I–II). Sin appears here not as guilt but as possession-by-defilement. The pollution behaves like a demon: it grips, it afflicts, it distorts.

This semi-personified portrayal is crucial for tracing the later biblical imagination. Sin is not simply what a person does. It is a force with its own gravity, capable of invading and acting upon the human being. It has agency—not absolute autonomy like Mōt in the Ugaritic

56

myths, but enough to behave in ways that resemble an independent power.

## Sin as Divine Residue or Mutated Agency

What makes this imagery especially striking is that Sin is understood to have a kind of divine origin. Not that Sin is good or sacred, but that it participates in the spiritual realm. Its potency comes from its proximity to the gods. In Sumerian city laments, disaster is a presence that settles over the people like a cloak, and the city's protective divine powers are said to depart—framing catastrophe as an invasive condition that makes life and divine protection unlivable (*Lament for Uruk*). The gods withdraw not because the sinner feels guilt or shame, but because Sin has made the environment inhospitable to their presence.

In this sense, sin is not simply immoral. It is dangerous. It inhabits spaces where the gods will no longer dwell. It compromises sanctity. It is, in the words of your broader thesis, a kind of "degraded divinity"—a corrupted residue of spiritual power that, when out of place, becomes monstrous.

## Sin as Demonic Force

In still other Mesopotamian texts, sin is explicitly linked with demonic affliction. Illness might be described as the hand of a deity or as the work of hostile powers resting heavily on the sufferer. Either way, the effect is the same: Sin is not an internal moral issue but an external force that invades the body. It is a foreign presence that must be expelled.

Here, again, ritual—not introspection—is the remedy. The priestly rites seek to cast out the malignant intruder through fire, water, smoke, and incantation. In other words, Sin must be exorcised.

## Sin as Foreign Invader

This broader cultural backdrop reveals why the biblical material will eventually portray sin in terms of burden, snare, pollutant, invader, and master. Israel did not invent these metaphors ex nihilo. They belonged to the cultural air of the ancient Near East. But Israel did something distinctive with them: it placed sin not in a fluid polytheistic cosmos but under the sovereignty of YHWH. Sin is not another god, nor a rival deity, but a force that operates within God's world as a distortion—a parasite feeding on what God made good.

This allows Sin to function within Israel's theology as a quasi-agent, a being that moves through bodies and spaces, accumulating, clinging, and infiltrating. And just as Mesopotamia developed rituals for removal,

Israel too will develop a sacrificial and priestly system for purging Sin—not because Sin is simply illegal, but because it is spiritually toxic.

### Bridge to Israel

With this backdrop in place, Israel's language about Sin becomes legible. The biblical writers speak of Sin as something that can be borne (Leviticus 10:17), transferred (Leviticus 16:21), cling (Psalm 38:4), increase (Genesis 15:16), or inscribed on the heart (Jeremiah 17:1). In speaking this way, they are drawing from a worldview in which Sin is not primarily moral but material, and where this *thing* is not primarily behavioral but invasive.

Before we turn to the Hebrew terms themselves—*ḥaṭṭā't, 'āwōn*, and their relatives—we must keep this conceptual world firmly in view. Otherwise, modern readers will domesticate the biblical language into the moral categories we already know. Sin in Scripture is too active, too burdensome, too mobile, too hostile to be safely contained in the narrow frame of "moral failure."

The ancient world teaches us the first and most important lesson: Sin is not merely wrong. Sin is alive. This ancient worldview is important because it is here where the ancient Israelites thought about, imagined, and came to understand the ideas that we find in Scripture.

## ḤAṬṬĀ'T AND 'ĀWŌN: ISRAEL'S SIN-COMPLEX

When we turn from the ancient Near East to Israel's Scriptures, we encounter a vocabulary for sin that is far more dynamic and multidimensional than modern moral categories can accommodate. The Hebrew words *ḥaṭṭā't* and *'āwōn*—the two most prominent terms for "sin"—do not function like entries in a theological dictionary. They behave more like forces, substances, and conditions. They move, cling, weigh down, accumulate, and can even be carried or transferred from one being to another. Modern interpreters often try cleanly to define them—*ḥaṭṭā't* as "sin offering" or "offense," *'āwōn* as "iniquity" or "guilt," and so forth. However, the texts themselves defy such narrow, modern categorization. These words occupy an entire semantic field rather than discrete theological categories, reflecting Israel's conviction that Sin is not simply an action but an ongoing state, a burden, and an active agent.

### Two Words, Many Forms: How Ḥaṭṭā't and 'Āwōn Shift Roles

The term *ḥaṭṭā't* itself illustrates this complexity. In Genesis 4:7, its earliest appearance, it clearly refers to an entity—"Sin is crouching at the door" (*lappetah ḥaṭṭā't rōvēṣ*)—a living presence with desire and intention. Yet in Leviticus, the same word denotes both the defiling condition left by wrongdoing (Leviticus 4:3) and the sacrificial ritual meant to purge that defilement (Leviticus 5:6; 6:25–30). The offering itself becomes *ḥaṭṭā't*, as though Sin's residue is absorbed by the sacrificial body and removed through its death.

Likewise, *'āwōn*, often rendered "iniquity," can describe the act of wrongdoing (Genesis 44:16), the condition or burden that results from misbehavior (Psalm 38:4), or even the punishment that flows from it (2 Kings 7:9). In Exodus 34:7, *'āwōn* is something God "bears away" (*nōsē' 'āwōn*), while in Leviticus 10:17 the priests themselves must "bear" (*lāsēt*) Israel's *'āwōn* by eating the purification offering. In both cases, Sin is imagined as a real, existential burden—a weight that must be lifted, carried, or transferred.

## Sin as Material Contaminant in the Imagination of Leviticus

This fluidity of meaning is not a linguistic accident but a theological insight. Sin in Israel's imagination is not a thin moral abstraction. It is a materializing reality with spatial and physical implications. It can reside on the body, settle into sacred objects, cling to garments, or infect the sanctuary itself. Leviticus presumes that even unintentional sins—actions done "in ignorance" (*bišgāgāh*)—produce residue that adheres to the sanctuary (Leviticus 4:2–3; 4:13; 16:16). Intent is irrelevant when dealing with contamination. As anthropologist Mary Douglas famously argued, impurity in ancient cultures reflects "matter out of place"—a failure of boundaries that threatens order itself (Douglas, 1966). Sin functions precisely in this way: it introduces disorder into the community and into the symbolic architecture of sacred life, demanding removal rather than explanation.

## Sin that Grows, Clings, Migrates, and Brands

This is why Israel's sin-vocabulary must be understood as a semantic complex rather than a tidy system. The words themselves behave as though Sin is a substance—one that can grow ("the iniquity of the Amorites is not yet complete," Genesis 15:16), cling ("my iniquities have passed over my head," Psalm 38:4), penetrate ("sin engraved on their hearts," Jeremiah 17:1), and migrate from one host to another ("he shall bear their iniquity," Leviticus 10:17; "Aaron shall lay the sins on the head of the goat," Leviticus 16:21). Sin travels. Sin accumulates. Sin burdens. Sin brands. These are not metaphors of psychology—they are descriptions of a contaminant with agency.

## The Day of Atonement as Expulsion Ritual

The Levitical material especially underscores this material aspect of Sin. In Leviticus 4, the repeated refrain is that the sanctuary must be purified "because of the sins of the people" (vv. 2, 13, 22, 27). The sanctuary becomes contaminated because Sin has a physical footprint. The High Priest must daub blood on the horns of the altar and sprinkle blood toward the veil—not because God requires spectacle, but because sin has left a stain on sacred space. As Jacob Milgrom has shown, this is not a system concerned with placating divine wrath, as modern Christian theology widely supposes, so much as containing and expelling impurity (Milgrom, 1991). Sin is a pollutant, not merely a fault, so its removal is a matter of cosmic hygiene.

The Day of Atonement in Leviticus 16 brings this logic to its climax. On that day, the high priest transfers Israel's accumulated "transgressions" (ʿăwōnōt), "rebellions" (pešāʾîm), and "sins" (ḥaṭṭāʾt) upon the head of the scapegoat (v. 21), who then carries the nation's Sin "to a remote place" (ʾerets gezerāh, v. 22). The goat is not simply symbolic. It is treated as a host for the nation's Sin—a carrier organism sent into the wilderness, the realm of demons and divine absence. What Israel has done—its Sin—is not forgiven in the modern sense. It is expelled. This ritual mirrors ancient Mesopotamian practices in the Šurpu and Maqlū series, where evil and Sin are spoken to, cursed, placed onto substitute objects or animals, and driven into liminal spaces away from the community (Šurpu II; Maqlū I–VIII). Israel uses this same imagery but reframes it under YHWH's sovereignty. The wilderness is not neutral—it is the domain to which Sin belongs. The camp is purged, and the contaminant is banished.

## Sin as Rival Power in Competition with the Divine Order

Given this conceptual world, it should not surprise us that the Hebrew vocabulary refuses strict compartmentalization. The same word can denote act, burden, effect, presence, and ritual because sin itself is all of these. Israel is not confused; Israel is describing the behavior of sin. As Jon Levenson notes, biblical writers consistently portray evil not as abstract disobedience but as "a power that competes with and opposes the divine order" (Levenson, 1988). Sin belongs to that constellation of anti-creation forces alongside Death, Sheol, and the chaotic deep. It is not a psychological category or failure of willpower. It is a rival presence.

## Why This Vocabulary Matters

This is why, before moving into specific texts, we must treat *ḥaṭṭā't* and *'āwōn* as indicators of a larger reality rather than as lexical units to be tightly defined. These words gesture toward a phenomenon that Israel experiences as living—sometimes crouching like a beast (Genesis 4:7), sometimes spreading like mold (Leviticus 13), sometimes entangling like cords (Proverbs 5:22), sometimes engraving itself into human hearts (Jeremiah 17:1). The language behaves as fluidly as the force it describes. And because the words operate in such diverse contexts— legal, ritual, poetic, prophetic—they give us a window into a worldview in which Sin is not what humans do but what dwells within them.

## Reading Sin as a Living Power

Thus, in what follows, we will not artificially divide Israel's vocabulary, but we'll trace its patterns of behavior. We'll examine how Sin crouches, clings, contaminates, ensnares, blinds, and brands. In short, we will read sin not as misstep but as monster—a power that behaves with unsettling autonomy and seeks again and again to occupy the self.

## SIN AS CROUCHING BEAST: GENESIS 4:7

Genesis 4:7 is one of the most theologically dense verses in the Hebrew Bible, and arguably the most important passage for understanding sin as an active, invasive, quasi-personal force. Long before Israel has rituals for expelling Sin, or prophets describing its grip on the human heart, Scripture gives us a scene of a monster waiting just outside a human door. The story of Cain is not merely a tale of jealousy and homicide. It is the Bible's first attempt to describe "sin" not only as something humans do but as something that acts upon humans. And the portrait it provides is thoroughly monstrous.

The divine warning to Cain reads:

> If you do well, will you not be accepted? And if you do not do well, Sin is crouching at the door (*lappetaḥ ḥaṭṭā't rōvēṣ*). Its desire is for you (*wě'ēlekha tešūqātō*), but you must rule over it (*wě'attā timšol-bō*, Genesis 4:7).

The key terms here demand attention. The word for "sin," *ḥaṭṭā't*, is grammatically feminine but functions here as a personified being with intentions and passions. Nothing in the narrative prepares the reader for this sudden appearance of *ḥaṭṭā't* as a living creature. It has no origin story, no genealogy, no description of its creation. It simply exists—already crouching, already hungry, already poised. The Hebrew verb *rōvēṣ*, "crouching," is the same verb used for animals lying in wait, often predatory (cf. Genesis 49:9; Job 38:40). It evokes a beast ready to spring, not a passive danger but an active one. The imagery is not of a stumble or slip but of an ambush.

This "crouching" Sin stands at the door (*lappetaḥ*), a threshold term that carries profound symbolic weight. In the ancient world, the doorway was a vulnerable liminal space—neither inside nor outside—where threats were most likely to appear. Demons in Mesopotamian incantations frequently lurk in the gate or at the threshold, attempting to infiltrate the home or body (*Maqlū* VII; *Šurpu* III). Israel, without adopting Mesopotamian demonology, preserves the same intuition, insisting that the greatest danger is not yet inside, but it is waiting to cross the boundary. Cain is not shown as a morally conflicted man deliberating over right and wrong. He is shown as someone with a monster outside his house.

### A Desire That Mirrors Eden

Equally striking is the clause "its desire is for you" (*wě'ělekā tešūqātō*). The construction echoes Genesis 3:16, where the woman's *tešūqāh* is directed toward her husband. The parallel is not accidental. In both cases, the phrase describes a force that seeks to master or dominate the other. The verb "desire" here connotes not affection but aggression—the urge to overcome, to possess, to consume. The monster of *ḥaṭṭā't* wants Cain, not in an emotional sense, but in the sense that a predator wants its prey.

God's counter-command—"but you must rule it" (*wě'attāh timšol-bō*)—invokes the language of mastery and dominion, the same language given to humanity over creation in Genesis 1:28. Sin is not simply a temptation to be resisted; it is a creature seeking dominion that must itself be subdued. The anthropological implication is enormous: Cain becomes the first human addressed as one who must exercise dominion not over animals or land but over a spiritual intruder that aims to seize him.

### A Monster Without a Backstory

The narrative leaves the reader with a crucial tension: Where did this thing come from? Unlike the serpent in Genesis 3—whose identity, though mysterious, is narratively introduced—*ḥaṭṭā't* simply appears. There is no causal chain. No mention of prior wrongdoing generating its presence. No suggestion that Cain "harbored" sin internally before this moment. The image is external and sudden: sin is already at the door. This absence of an origin story reinforces the text's portrayal of sin as an invasive force, not reducible to psychological impulse or moral weakness. Sin is not born from Cain; sin seeks to enter Cain.

The literary effect is chilling. The reader encounters a creature that behaves like Mōt in Ugaritic myth (KTU 1.4; 1.5)—a being of appetite and inevitability—yet it is not treated as a deity. Nor is it a free-floating cosmic monster. It is something that comes to human beings, something that seeks entry, something that appropriates the threshold of the human life. The text locates Sin at the edge of human agency, not at its center—a danger not yet inside the self but imminently crossing over.

## The First Portrait of Spiritual Predation

If we take the narrative seriously on its own terms, Sin in Genesis 4:7 is better described as a predator than as a moral abstraction. It is a being whose posture is already aggressive, whose appetite has already awakened, and whose target has already been chosen. Cain's ensuing murder of Abel is therefore not portrayed as a simple lapse in judgment. It is the consequence of a failed confrontation between human agency and a hostile spiritual entity.

Cain does not simply fall into *sin*—he is overpowered by *Sin*. The narrative's psychological depth lies not in Cain's emotions but in the unseen battle at his door. The text invites us to imagine Cain with a monster leaning against the threshold of his life, waiting for him to falter. When he does, the monster enters and takes over. Later biblical reflections on Sin's ensnaring, contaminating, or possessing qualities all trace back to this moment. Genesis 4:7 is the Bible's first articulation of Sin as a living force, and everything that follows in Israel's Scriptures develops this portrayal rather than refuting it.

## Threshold Horror and the Human Condition

Genesis 4:7 is the ancient equivalent of discovering that the danger is not somewhere out in the world but already on your doorstep. Like a creature in the shadows beyond a porch light, Sin is near, watching, waiting. The danger is not distant but proximate; not generalized but personal. Cain's life is not invaded by an impulse but by an entity.

What the modern reader must grasp is that Genesis 4:7 does not depict Sin metaphorically as a beast. It identifies Sin's behavior as beastlike, predatory, parasitic, and invasive. The metaphor works precisely because it reflects a deeper ontology: Sin behaves like a creature because Sin is treated as one. Not a god, not a demon, not an abstract force, but a monstrous presence that must be mastered or else will master.

## SIN AS CONTAGION IN THE RITUAL EXORCISM OF LEVITICUS

If Genesis 4 introduces Sin as a crouching beast, Leviticus develops a complementary portrait of Sin as a contaminant, a force that spreads, clings, corrupts, and accumulates until it must be violently purged. Modern readers often associate Leviticus with moral laws or ritual fastidiousness, but the book's underlying logic is far more dynamic. Sin in Leviticus is not primarily about "guilt feelings" or "bad behavior." It is about spiritual pollution, a defiling substance or presence that has the power to permeate human bodies, material objects, communal spaces, and even the sanctuary of God.

This portrayal aligns closely with ancient Near Eastern ritual theory, where impurity was not simply symbolic but ontologically real—a dangerous residue requiring expulsion. As Mary Douglas famously argued, impurity in the ancient world was matter out of place (1966). Leviticus extends this intuition into the theological realm. Sin is not dirt accidentally misplaced. It is a foreign invader that disorients the world God ordered. It must be removed, not excused.

### Sin as Ontological Residue

Consider the repeated refrain in Leviticus 4:

> If anyone sins unintentionally… (wĕ-ī'm nepeš kī-teḥĕṭā' bišgāgāh, 27; cf. vv. 2, 13, 22).

These unintentional acts still require sacrifice—not because ignorance deserves punishment, but because the Sin has left something behind. The vocabulary of ḥaṭṭā't ("sin") and 'āwōn ("iniquity, guilt burden") makes this clear: these are not words for mistakes. Rather, they are names for conditions or energies that adhere. Sin behaves like mold in a house (cf. Leviticus 14), like mildew in garments, like a stain on the altar. It is persistent and transmissive.

The logic is thus material, not simply moralistic. If a priest sins "thus bringing guilt on the people" (Leviticus 4:3), the act is not a bad example as much as it is an act that releases a contaminant, literally, upon the people. The people do not need to imitate the priest to be endangered by his condition. They are endangered by this condition because that's what Sin does: it pollutes and spreads until it is finally eradicated. Pollution in the biblical imagination spreads like radiation. As such, it does not require willing participation. It simply requires proximity. In other words, I don't have to participate in the misdeed in order to be tarnished by it.

## Sin that Attaches to Objects, Bodies, and Sacred Space

Leviticus treats Sin as something capable of clinging to the very architecture of Israel's world. In Leviticus 16:16, the priest is commanded to apply blood to the horns of the altar "to purge the sanctuary from the impurity of the people" (*wěkhippēr 'al-haqqōdeš miṭṭum'ōt bǝnê Yiśrā'ēl*). The sanctuary itself has absorbed Israel's impurity. Sin behaves like a pollutant that seeps into the walls.

This imagery reaches its climax in Leviticus 16, where the Day of Atonement ritual presupposes that the entire tabernacle has, over time, become saturated. Verse 16 states plainly that the High Priest must cleanse the shrine "because of the impurities of the Israelites, and because of their transgressions, all their sins." The impurities are already there, like accumulated dust or soot. Sin is not a momentary misdeed but a spiritual residue that builds up and must be removed before it renders the sanctuary uninhabitable.

It is no coincidence that Ezekiel 8–11 later depicts the Temple abandoned by YHWH due to gross contamination. Leviticus anticipates this reality: if Sin is allowed to accumulate, God leaves. Pollution is a theological threat. Indeed, it's an existential threat.

## The Day of Atonement: Israel's Annual Exorcism

Leviticus 16 is one of the most misunderstood ritual texts in Scripture because modern readers assume its primary purpose is forgiveness in the sense of pardon for misbehavior. But the text itself tells a different story. The Day of Atonement is a large-scale, enacted exorcism.

Two goats are used: one for purification (*kippēr*) of the sanctuary, and one to bear the sins of the people into the wilderness. The first goat's blood cleanses sacred space from contamination, and the second becomes a carrier for Israel's accumulated Sin, which must be cast out into the realm of chaos.

The priest lays hands upon the second goat and confesses "all the iniquities of the people of Israel" (Leviticus 16:21). The Hebrew is vivid:

He shall place them upon the head of the goat (*wěnātan 'ōtām 'al-rōš hassā'îr*).

Sin here is a transferable substance. It can be placed, borne, carried.

The goat is then sent "to Azazel" (*la'azā'zēl*) in the wilderness—a figure or location associated with the far edges of order. Scholars remain divided on Azazel's identity: a demon of the wasteland, a cliff or desolate place, or a symbolic representation of chaos (for discussion, see Milgrom, 1991; 2000; 2001). But this diversity in interpretation only highlights the core reality that Sin is not "forgiven" in the camp—it must be expelled from it. Ritual logic here is not judicial but cosmological. Sin functions like an entity that must be driven out of the community into the realm where such entities belong.

In other words, Israel does not merely apologize on the Day of Atonement. Israel performs a purge.

## Leviticus and the Logic of Contagion

The way Leviticus treats Sin mirrors ancient Mesopotamian incantation traditions, where impurity and wrongdoing were removed by ritual force. In the *Maqlū* texts, the sufferer cries out for the removal of evil affecting the body or wrongdoing that adheres (*Maqlū* VII–VIII). Priests use burning, washing, smoke, and symbolic transfers to cleanse the afflicted. The verb forms are aggressive: crush, burn, scatter, exile.

Leviticus adopts similar ritual grammar but reframes it under the sovereignty of YHWH. The logic remains recognizably ancient: Sin is something that attaches, invades, and must be driven away. But Israel's innovation is theological rather than procedural. Impurity is not simply cosmic misalignment, but it is defilement of YHWH's dwelling. What contaminates the sanctuary jeopardizes Israel's vocation as a people among whom God dwells (cf. Exodus 25:8).

This fusion of ancient Near Eastern ritual logic with Israelite theology yields a uniquely powerful depiction of Sin. It is not merely "breaking the rules," nor mere "personal guilt." It is a spiritual pollutant saturating the camp, threatening the divine presence, and requiring dramatic expulsion. Sin is not something one chooses. It is something that chooses, attaches, corrupts, and forces God's people into defensive ritual action.

## Exorcism by Proxy

When we look at the Day of Atonement through these lenses, the ritual resembles less a courtroom and more the climax of a horror narrative. The creature that has lived among the people all year—the crouching thing from Genesis 4—has infiltrated the sanctuary. It must be extracted. The priest does not punish Sin—he banishes it. The goat does not pay a penalty—it carries out an invader.

This is why I describe the ritual as exorcism by proxy. Israel does not cast out demons. Instead, Israel casts out Sin itself, the invasive presence that has lodged in bodies, garments, houses, and most shockingly, in the sanctuary of God. Every year, the monster is driven back into the wilderness—but like all monsters of ancient lore, it returns. Hence the cycle.

*Sin as Contagion in Israel's Ritual Imagination*

When Leviticus is read in this light, we see that its ritual system offers one of the clearest articulations of Sin not as misdeed but as entity. It behaves like contagion, spreads like contamination, and requires purgation. And in a manner parallel to Death's devouring appetite, Sin displays in these texts a kind of instinct: to cling, to grow, to saturate, to corrupt space until God's presence is forced out. It is a monster not from mythic seas, but from within Israel's camp.

## SIN AS HUNTER AND SNARE: WISDOM AND PSALMIC IMAGERY

If Leviticus shows Sin behaving like contagion that clings to bodies and space, the Psalms and Wisdom literature tilt the camera to another angle. Here, Sin behaves like a hunter. It stalks, pursues, lays traps, tightens cords. The language is not that of vague "moral struggle," but of pursuit and capture. And importantly, this hunting imagery overlaps with what we saw in the Death chapter, even as it pushes in a distinct direction: Death is the hunter that closes in from beyond, while Sin is the hunter whose snares can be woven into the very life of the one it captures.

### Drowning Beneath Iniquity: Psalm 38's Burdened Sufferer

Psalm 38 gives one of the most evocative portraits. The psalmist laments, "For my iniquities have gone over my head" (*kī-'ăwōnōtay 'āverū ro'šī*), "like a heavy burden they are too heavy for me" (*kemassā' kāvēd yikbĕdū mimmennī*; Psalm 38:4). The idiom "have gone over my head" is not simply about feeling overwhelmed. It evokes drowning or submersion. The "iniquities" (*'āwōnōt*) do not just weigh on the conscience, but they rise like floodwaters, submerging the psalmist's head. The following phrase, "like a heavy burden," intensifies the point: the "burden" (*massā'*) is something placed on a person from the outside. In other words, Sin here is not merely "what I did." It has become a force that presses down, pins, and threatens to drag the sufferer under.

The verbs reinforce this dynamic. The *'ăwōnōt* "have passed over" (*'āvar*) his head and "make heavy" (*kāvēd*) upon him. The iniquity behaves like an external agent, not a private feeling. At a conceptual level, this is close to what we saw with Death's "cords" in Psalm 18 and 2 Samuel 22. Yet there, the cords of *māwet* and *še'ōl*—Death and Sheol—bind from the realm of the grave. Here, *'āwōn*—Sin—binds as something that belongs to the psalmist and yet moves and crushes with a life of its own.

*Caught in the Cords: Proverbs and the Mechanics of Capture*

Proverbs 5:22 sharpens the hunter imagery with technical language from the world of trapping:

> His own iniquities will capture the wicked, and he is held fast in the cords of his Sin (*ʿăwōnōtāw yilkeḏūnō ʾet-hārāšāʿ, ūvĕḥavlē ḥaṭṭāʾtō yittāmēk*).

The verb *lākaḏ* ("to capture, seize") is the standard term for catching prey in a net or snare. The wicked one (*hārāšāʿ*) does not simply "suffer consequences"—he is literally "caught" by his iniquities. The second colon intensifies the picture: he is "held" or "tethered" (*yittāmēk*) in the *ḥavlē ḥaṭṭāʾtō*—the "cords" or "ropes of his Sin." *Ḥevel* and its plural *ḥavlīm* are the same words used for measuring lines, ropes, and bindings. Hunters and fowlers in ancient Israel used nets (*rešet, mikmōret*), snares (*pāḥ, moqēš*), and cords (*ḥevel*) to immobilize animals before the kill. Proverbs 5 assumes this world, where Sin is imagined not as a feeling of guilt, but as a rope looped around the ankle that suddenly tightens.

The interplay of possessive forms is theologically rich. They are "his" iniquities and "his" Sin (*ʿăwōnōtāw, ḥaṭṭāʾtō*), yet these iniquities and this Sin are the hunters. They do the capturing. They do the binding. The text does not say, "his guilt makes him feel trapped." It says, "his iniquities capture him, and he is held fast." Agency is attributed to Sin. It moves toward the sinner with all the determination of a tracker closing in on quarry.

*The Pursuit Motif in Proverbs*

Proverbs 13:21 adds a further nuance, namely, that "Evil pursues sinners" (*ḥaṭṭāʾīm teraddēf rāʿāh*). The verb *rāḏap*—"to pursue, chase"—is frequently used of armies chasing defeated foes (e.g., Exodus 14:9) and of hostile enemies driving after someone's life (Psalm 7:1; 143:3). Here, *rāʿāh* ("evil") is not a static condition, as it pursues the "sinners" (*ḥaṭṭāʾīm*). In the conceptual world of Proverbs, Sin and "evil" (*rāʿāh*) overlap: wrongdoing is not merely what the wicked do, but it is what hunts them. The sinner is not leading evil around; evil is on their heels.

*Sin as Heavy, Cunning, and Relentless*

When you set Psalm 38:4, Proverbs 5:22, and Proverbs 13:21 alongside one another, a coherent portrait emerges. Sin is heavy enough to drown, cunning enough to lay snares, and relentless enough to chase.

The imagery is not tidy or purely metaphorical. It borrows from the lived experience of a world in which one could step into a hidden noose at any moment or feel an enemy closing the gap from behind. Sin is not simply an error to be regretted—it is a force that seeks to close, to bind, to overtake.

This helps explain why the Wisdom tradition is so insistent on vigilance. "Make level the path of your feet" (Proverbs 4:26), "do not enter the path of the wicked" (4:14), "keep your way far from her" (5:8). These exhortations assume a landscape littered with traps. The danger is not only that one might "decide badly," but that one might unwittingly step into a field of concealed snares. Sin's cords wait in the ordinary paths of life. The wise are not just morally upright. They are spiritually cautious because they know they move through hunted territory.

### Sin's Snares Versus Death's Cords

The same pattern we saw with Death's cords is at work here but folded inward. In Psalm 18, "the cords of Death" and "the torrents of Belial" come from beyond. They wrap around the psalmist's body from outside and pull him toward Sheol (Psalm 18:4–6). With Sin, the cords arise from what is "his"—'ăwōnōtāw, ḥaṭṭā'tō—yet once formed, they act as an autonomous snare. Death is the external hunter, while Sin is the hunter who manages to fashion snares out of the sinner's own iniquity. In that sense, the Wisdom literature is already gesturing toward the paradox Paul will later name when he cries that "it is no longer I who do it, but Sin that dwells within me" (Romans 7:17).

In Tolkien's *The Lord of the Rings*, Gollum is bound to the Ring not by a rational decision that he reconsiders each morning, but by a devotion that has hardened into chains. The Ring does not simply reflect his choices—it constrains them. Something he "owns" now owns him. Proverbs 5 imagines something similar: what begins as "his Sin" becomes the cords by which he is held. The possession reverses.

### Sin as Agent, Not Metaphor

Theologically, this imagery undercuts any attempt to reduce Sin to mere moralism. Sin in Psalms and Proverbs is not a tally of infractions. It is a power that stalks and captures. The sinner is culpable—these are his iniquities, his sins—but he is also genuinely ensnared. He is the agent who stepped into the trap and the victim now dangling from the snare. The language is doing both at once.

This is why the Wisdom tradition often pairs confession of guilt with cries for deliverance. The psalmist does not merely say, "I confess," as if he believes that he feels bad simple guilt or shame about his plight.

Rather, he pleads, "Deliver me from all my transgressions" (*mikkol-peša'ay haṣṣīlēnī*; Psalm 39:8). Sin is something from which one must be saved, not only something one must regret. The hunter motif makes this concrete: nets must be torn, cords cut, pursuit stopped. The sinner does not simply need enlightenment or new resolve. He needs someone stronger to break the bindings of his iniquity.

### The Hunter Inside the Self in Paul's Anthropology

By the time we reach Paul's language of being "sold under Sin" (*pepramenos hypo hamartian*, Romans 7:14) and being "captured by the Law of Sin" (7:23), the ground has already been laid. Israel's poems and proverbs have long imagined Sin as a hunter and snare, a force that closes in and constricts. Paul's analysis is more explicit and psychological, but it is not novel. He is giving doctrinal shape to an older picture: the cords of Sin tightening around a human life until only a stronger liberator can pull them free.

## SIN AS INVADER, BLINDER, AND BRANDER IN THE PROPHETS

If the Wisdom writings show Sin as a hunter and trapper, the prophets shift the imagery again. Now, Sin is not simply something one commits nor merely a snare in which one becomes caught. In the prophetic imagination, Sin becomes an invasive presence—something that enters, distorts, blinds, pollutes, and finally brands the human heart as its own.

The prophets do not treat Sin as a metaphor for guilt. Rather, they treat it as a force that desecrates sacred space, disrupts perception, and fundamentally disfigures human identity. The vocabulary and imagery they use suggest a sort of possession, infestation, and corruption—not in the sensational later sense of "demonic possession," but in the earlier biblical sense of ontological invasion of persons and community.

### Isaiah 6:10—The Parasite of Perception in Isaiah's Diagnosis

Isaiah's call narrative famously includes YHWH's command that the prophet "make the heart of this people dull, and their ears heavy, and blind their eyes" (Isaiah 6:10). The verbs are striking: *hašmēn* ("make fat, insensible"), *hakbēd* ("make heavy"), *hāša'* ("blind"). Modern readers often imagine this as mere metaphor, but in context Isaiah is naming a pathology. Israel's sensory faculties—heart, ears, eyes—are not simply deficient, but they are actually being acted upon. Something makes them dull, clogs their hearing, and blinds their sight.

The prophetic complaint elsewhere clarifies that this something is not God's arbitrary punishment but the consequence of entrenched sinfulness. Isaiah 1 frames Israel as a body sick "from head to foot" (Isaiah 1:6). The sickness is a sort of internal rot. Sin, for Isaiah, is a parasite on the faculties of perception. It prevents the people from perceiving God's actions, from seeing justice, and from hearing the prophetic word—hence "they do not understand" (Isaiah 1:3). Sin is more than simple ignorance. It is a crippling infestation of the very organs designed to respond to God.

This is why Isaiah often pairs language of Sin with that of sensory malfunction. In Isaiah 44:18, we read that idolaters "do not know, nor do they understand, for he has plastered their eyes so they cannot see, and their hearts so they cannot understand." The verb *ṭāḥ* ("to plaster over") evokes both ritual smearing and physical obstruction. The idols do not blind their makers, but instead Sin, through idolatry, blinds them. Isaiah's portrait is therefore not that of an intellectual mistake but a spiritual seizure of sensory capacity. Sin has moved inside the perceptual apparatus and taken control.

### Ezekiel 8–11—The Polluted Temple in Ezekiel's Vision of Infestation

If Isaiah shows Sin invading the body's "senses," Ezekiel shows it invading sacred space itself. Ezekiel 8–11 is one of the most terrifying sequences in the Hebrew Bible, not because of explicit violence but because of what Sin does to the Temple. Ezekiel is taken in a vision to Jerusalem, where he witnesses a series of abominations: images of creeping things and detestable beasts painted on the walls (Ezekiel 8:10), women weeping for Tammuz (8:14), men bowing to the sun in the Temple court (8:16). Each scene reveals a deeper infestation of idolatry inside the very place meant to host YHWH's glory.

What is striking is how Ezekiel narrates this as progressive contamination. It is not simply that Israel is guilty of *sins*. Rather, *Sin* has entered the Temple, proliferated in its chambers, and rendered it uninhabitable. The climax is devastating: "the glory of YHWH went up from the cherub... to the threshold of the house" (Ezekiel 9:3), then later departs entirely to the Mount of Olives (Ezekiel 11:23). God is driven out not by external threat but by internal pollution. Sin has taken residence inside sacred architecture.

This is not mere metaphorical moralism. In Ezekiel's symbolic economy, the Temple is the heart of Israel, the locus of divine-human communion. When Sin invades the Temple, it has invaded the collective body. When YHWH's glory departs, the people are left spiritually vacant. Ezekiel thus portrays Sin as a kind of Temple-infesting

71

monster—an unclean presence that colonizes holy space until the divine presence can no longer remain.

### Jeremiah 17:1—Jeremiah's Terrifying Image of Engraved Ownership

Jeremiah brings the prophetic critique down to its most intimate and disturbing level. "The Sin of Judah is written with an iron pen. With a diamond point it is engraved on the tablet of their heart" (Jeremiah 17:1). Few texts in Scripture capture the invasive nature of Sin more graphically. Here, Sin is not external pollutant (as in Leviticus) nor crouching beast (as in Genesis 4) nor hunter (as in Wisdom). Sin is a hand holding an iron stylus, carving itself into the human heart.

The verbs here are critically important. *Ketuvah* ("written") evokes the recording of official documents. But Jeremiah goes further: Sin is not merely "written"—it is "engraved" (*ḥārūšāh*) with a "diamond point" (*ṣippōren šāmīr*). The heart (*lēv*) is described as a *luaḥ*, a "tablet of stone." Jeremiah depicts a horrifying inversion of Sinai: instead of God's covenant written on stone tablets, Sin writes its own anti-covenant onto the human heart.

This engraving is not imagery for guilt—it is imagery for ownership. The heart bears Sin's mark, and the person belongs to what has inscribed itself there. Later prophetic hope (Jeremiah 31:33; Ezekiel 36:26–27) reverses this by promising a new heart and a divine inscription, but Jeremiah's diagnosis remains: Sin brands its host like a master branding cattle. The heart becomes the site of subjugation, as Sin has become the master of the human self.

### The Horror Image Behind the Prophets

In vampire lore, the bitten victim bears the mark of the one who feeds on them. The bite is not simply wound but signature, designating the victim as property. Jeremiah's iron stylus functions with similar symbolic force: Sin marks the heart as its possession.

Likewise, the Ringwraith imagery from Tolkien works quietly in the background. Their humanity erodes when they accept the Ring's inscription of power. Their "seeing" becomes distorted, and they exist as shadows of themselves. That is precisely Jeremiah's and Isaiah's concern: Sin does not merely evoke guilt—it corrodes personhood and perception from within.

### A Theology of Eviction: When Sin Drives Out God

Across these prophetic portraits, a consistent pattern emerges. Sin functions as an invader that takes up residence in people and places, twisting perception and desecrating what is holy. In Isaiah, Sin invades the senses, making the people unable to perceive God. In Ezekiel, Sin invades the Temple, driving God's glory away. In Jeremiah, Sin invades the heart, engraving itself into the very core of identity.

These texts converge on a sobering theological insight. Sin is not simply humanity turning from God. It is a power that turns humanity into a space where God cannot dwell. Nor does Sin simply lead to divine judgment. It creates the conditions in which divine presence becomes unsustainable.

This explains why prophetic calls to repentance almost always involve imagery of cleansing, healing, and heart renovation rather than mere intellectual correction. The problem is not incorrect doctrine but invasive corruption.

### From External Invasion to Internal Tyranny

By the time we reach Paul, the prophetic imagery provides a foundation for understanding Sin as an indwelling tyrant. Romans 1–3 echoes Isaiah's blindness and dullness, and Romans 7 vividly enacts Jeremiah's image of Sin writing itself into the inner person. The departure of God's glory in Ezekiel becomes the Pauline logic of exile from God's presence and restoration through the Spirit.

The prophetic texts therefore form the bridge between early portrayals of Sin as a crouching beast and Paul's radical portrayal of Sin as an internal ruler. Before Paul can describe the human being as a "slave to Sin" (Romans 6:17, 20) or as someone in whom "sin dwells" (*hamartia oikousa en emoi*, Romans 7:17), we must see the groundwork the prophets have laid. Sin has already become an invader, a blinder, a polluter, and a brander long before Paul gives it a name as enslaving Power.

The prophets thus contribute something essential to the Bible's monster-grammar: Sin is not merely what we do; it is something that comes to dwell in us, distort us, brand us, and estrange us from the presence of God. It turns bodies into unseeing vessels, hearts into engraved tablets, and sanctuaries into desecrated ruins. And with that realization, Paul's language of Sin as a tyrannical indweller will sound less like theological innovation and more like the final form of a terrifying pattern that began centuries before his lifetime.

## THE MONSTER WITHIN: SIN'S POSSESSION AND THE POROUS SELF

One of the challenges in writing about biblical "possession" is that our imaginations quickly leap to demons, spinning heads, or late-medieval exorcism tropes. But the biblical writers reach for something far subtler, and in many ways far more frightening: the idea that a hostile power can work inside a person—co-opting desires, rerouting perception, bending agency—without ever manifesting as a visible creature.

Modern biology actually gives us a window into this ancient way of imagining spiritual invasion. One of my favorite examples from science is the Ophiocordyceps fungus. This is a fungus found in places like the Amazon, where its spores, upon entering into a host insect, infest it and take over its body. It's known for creating the infamous Zombie Ant. When the ant descends to the rainforest floor, it picks up spores from the fungus. From here, the spores enter into the ant, and once inside the host, the organism slowly colonizes the ant's nervous system. It takes over the ant to the point where it alters its perception and reroutes its behavior so thoroughly that the insect's movements cease to be its own. The creature is still alive, still recognizably an ant, but its actions now serve the invading fungus.

Ancient people did not need microscopy to imagine such things. For them, certain forces—diseases, curses, demons, or in our case Sin— already behaved like invading agents that seized the body or the will. In that sense, Ophiocordyceps is a biological example of what the ancient world already knew: the self is porous, and hostile powers can dwell within it. Sin, in biblical thought, is precisely such a power.

Here, we have brought together two trajectories that permeate Israel's Scriptures: Sin as an internal occupier (a possessing agent) and the human as a temple-like, porous self that can host either YHWH or rival powers. These are not two different ideas but two sides of the same theological claim. Sin is not merely what we do. Sin is what uses us to do itself. And the human being is not merely a moral subject. The human is a site—an outer temple and inner sanctuary—where powers contend for residence.

### The Human as Porous Temple Open to Occupation

All of this brings us to a crucial anthropological point: the human being in biblical thought is not a sealed, autonomous individual but a porous self, open to the presence of God or rival powers. The creation story already signals this. Humans are formed from dust (*'āfār*) yet animated by God's divine breath (*nĕšāmā*, Genesis 2:7). They are earth-creatures infused with divine life, neither merely material nor purely spiritual. This hybrid ontology makes them capable of extraordinary glory—but it also leaves them vulnerable to infiltration.

The temple imagery reinforces the point. If the cosmos is God's temple, and the human microcosm is likewise temple-shaped, then the

74

human interior is not neutral space but sacred architecture. The "heart" is a sort of holy of holies (Putthoff, 2017). Desire is an altar. Memory is a storehouse. Imagination, speech, and will are ritual instruments. For this reason, Sin never merely affects people. It inhabits them. It moves through the channels of thought, desire, memory, and habit. It attaches itself to rituals of life, shaping patterns of action and reaction.

This is why Israel's Scriptures do not speak about Sin as if it were only a moral slip. They speak as if Sin were a tenant, a squatter, a parasite, or a rival deity's emissary. The porous structure of the human person—open to wind, spirit, breath, thought, word—creates the very conditions under which Sin can then act as invader.

### When Sin Takes the Throne: The Inversion of Agency

Once Sin enters the human interior, the biblical writers consistently describe a frightening inversion: the human acts, but their action is no longer fully theirs. Hosea speaks of people whose deeds are "entangled" (Hosea 5:4). Proverbs describes sinners who are "held fast in the cords of their sin" (Proverbs 5:22). Psalm 38 laments a force that rises "over my head" (*'al-rō'šī*, Psalm 38:4), drowning the psalmist's agency in its depth.

At this point, the Ophiocordyceps fungus and Zombie Ant analogy becomes especially illuminating. The insect that this fungus invades is not dead. It still moves. But its behavior is no longer its own. Everything that the Zombie Ant does is under the control of the Ophiocordyceps fungus. The biblical anthropology of Sin is strikingly similar. People under Sin's sway do not stop acting—but instead of behaving of their own volition, they act consistently with the desires of the occupier. Their agency persists, but it is bent. Their choices remain real, yet constricted, habituated, re-routed by something that has taken root within.

This prepares us for Paul's later articulation of the same dynamic: "I do not understand my own actions... I do not do the good I want, but the evil I do not want is what I do" (Romans 7:15–19). Whatever we make of the identity of the "I" in Romans 7, the description is consistent with Israel's earlier imagery: Sin becomes an indwelling tyrant (*hē oikousa en emoi hamartia*, Romans 7:17).

### From Occupation to Exorcism in Paul's Letters

By the end of the Hebrew Bible, Sin is not just crouching at the door or clinging to the sanctuary. It has become something like a personal interior presence, engraving itself on the heart, blinding the senses, colonizing sacred space, redirecting desire, and hijacking human agency. In this anthropology, the human being is not a neutral chooser but a sacred site overrun.

This is exactly where the biblical story turns from anthropology to soteriology—or from a story about human nature (anthropology) to a story about salvation (soteriology). If the human temple is occupied by hostile presence, then what is needed is not new moral effort but a stronger indwelling power. Paul will make it explicit that the Spirit must dwell where Sin seeks to dwell (Romans 8:9–11). The exorcism must happen from the inside out.

Thus, this section brings us to the threshold of Paul's theology. Before Paul can speak of the Spirit filling the heart, he must describe Sin as already dwelling there. Before he can speak of liberation, he must narrate enslavement. Before "life in the Spirit" can be a possibility, the Scriptures must portray life under an indwelling tyrant. And they do.

In every metaphor we've traced—whether the crouching predator, contaminating agent, snare-setting hunter, blinding force, or heart-engraving occupier—the logic is the same. Sin is not simply what humans commit. Rather, it is a monstrous presence that commits its will through humans. It is an invader, a possessor, and a usurper of sacred space. And the human self, porous and temple-formed, is the battleground.

Which is why, as we move toward Paul, the question shifts from "How can humans stop sinning?" to "Who can evict Sin from its dwelling-place?" Paul will answer with the only solution Scripture ever envisions: a stronger Spirit, a new indwelling presence, a reclaimed temple.

## SUMMARY: SIN AS THE BIBLE'S INVASIVE MONSTER

Across Israel's Scriptures, Sin emerges not as a private moral lapse but as a living, invasive force—an inner counterpart to the outer predations of Death. Where Death stalks creation from without, Sin crouches at the threshold of the self, seeking entry (Genesis 4:7). Its earliest biblical appearance already signals its nature, namely, that it is a creature with posture, appetite, and intent. And once inside, Sin does not simply accuse; it occupies.

Israel's lexical world reinforces this agency. Terms such as *ḥaṭṭā't* and *'āwōn* describe not only actions but burdens that grow, cling, and require removal. Leviticus presents Sin as something transferable, accumulative, and contaminating—an ontological pollutant that necessitates ritual expulsion, not moral self-correction. Wisdom and psalmic traditions portray it as a hunter whose cords tighten around its prey (Proverbs 5:22). The prophets expose its deeper work of blinding the senses (Isaiah 6:10), infesting sacred space (Ezekiel 8–11), and engraving its mark upon the heart (Jeremiah 17:1). Step by step, Scripture reveals a power that moves from crouching outside the house to dwelling within its rooms.

Taken together, these portraits converge on a single reality. Sin is a rival presence that seeks embodiment. It is parasitic rather than creative, deforming rather than generating, a counterfeit indwelling that twists the vessel it inhabits. The human being—hybrid of dust and divine breath—is uniquely vulnerable to this invasion, capable of becoming sanctuary or battleground, image or idol.

As we close out this chapter, we see the way Sin stands revealed as the Bible's other great chaos monster. It is not merely what humans do, but it is what can take up residence in them. In the next chapter, Paul will name this creature explicitly, describe its occupation of the self with disarming clarity, and announce the only power strong enough to displace it.

# CHAPTER 5—MONSTROUS HUMANITY IN ROMANS 5–8

## SIN AND DEATH IN PAUL'S WRITINGS

Few passages in Scripture are as psychologically raw or theologically dense as Romans 7:7–25. It is the most haunting portrait of the human self in all of Paul's writings—a confession not of weakness, but of possession. Contrary to the way so many teachers, preachers, and interpreters have understood this text, the apostle does not describe a man making bad choices or wrestling with guilt. He describes a self divided, occupied, torn open by powers greater than its will (Käsemann, 1971; 1994; Gaventa, 2004; 2011; 2016; 2024). The vocabulary is intimate and terrifying. He speaks of Sin and Death not as abstractions, but as predators, squatters, and rulers that have taken up residence in the human body (Käsemann, 1971; Gaventa, 2011; 2016; 2024).

To read this passage rightly—and the whole of Romans 5–8—we have to suspend our modern instincts. Western readers, shaped by centuries of moral theology and post-Enlightenment psychology, tend to interpret Romans 7 as the drama of conscience: the good self that wants to obey God but can't quite manage it. But Paul's language resists that flattening. He is not diagnosing neurosis or moral frustration. He is describing a haunted temple—a human body invaded by powers it cannot evict (Dunn, 1975; Gaventa, 2011; 2016; cf. Schweitzer, 1931).

This kind of language makes sense in Paul's world more than ours. He is not writing as a modern ethicist or a Greek dualist but as a man steeped in the cosmology of the ancient Near East, in which spiritual powers were personal, embodied, and territorial—active within both the spiritual and the physical realms (Schweitzer, 1931; Käsemann, 1971; Martyn, 1997). As we saw above, in the ancient world, Sin was not merely a legal infraction. It was a force that clung, defiled, and spread like contagion (cf. Leviticus 4–16; Wright, 2013; Gaventa, 2024). Death (*māwet* in Hebrew, *thanatos* in Greek) was not simply mortality—it was a devouring force with a mouth, a crown, and an appetite. These were living powers, rivals to life itself.

Paul's claim, shocking in its simplicity, is that these powers now live in us. The monsters of the old myths—the serpent of Eden, the beast of Sheol, the devourer Māwet—have moved inward (cf. Käsemann, 1994). What the ancient world imagined at the edges of creation or in the nether spaces of the community, Paul locates within the chest and head of every human being. The battlefield has shifted from sea and sky to soul and body. The *Chaoskampf*—the war between order and chaos, between God and the forces of uncreation—now unfolds in human flesh (Käsemann, 1994).

This is why Romans 5–8 must be read slowly, almost like a horror text. The verbs throb with animation: Sin "seizes," "deceives," "kills," "dwells." The Law "provokes." Death "reigns." These are not metaphors of psychology. They are the grammar of invasion. Paul's syntax breaks under the strain, collapsing into paradox: "It is no longer I who do it, but Sin dwelling in me" (7:17). The Greek word for "dwelling"—*oikeō*—means to reside, to take up (permanent) lodging (Gaventa, 2004; 2016; 2024). This is the vocabulary of habitation, of gods and spirits moving into temples (Gorman, 2009; Martin, 2014). Paul's "I" (*egō*) is no longer an autonomous self but a contested space.

Scholars have wrestled for decades to make sense of this haunting monologue. Rudolf Bultmann (1948) read it as an existential conflict between the authentic and inauthentic self. Ernst Käsemann (1971; 1994) turned the discussion in a more mythic direction, arguing that Paul's "Sin" is a cosmic power. Since then, interpreters from E. P. Sanders (1977) to N. T. Wright (2013) and Douglas Campbell (2009) have debated what Paul's "I" represents. Emma Wasserman (2007) has proposed that Paul here uses Middle Platonic psychology, and Joseph Longarino (2021) emphasizes Sin's persistence within embodied believers. Jamie Davies (2022) argues that Romans 5–8 holds together both forensic justice (law and guilt) and cosmic deliverance (liberation from powers), not as competitors but as complementary levels of analysis. Beverly Gaventa has gone to great lengths to show that Sin and Death in Romans 5–8 must be viewed as enslaving powers or forces from which Christ has liberated humanity, and her work should be foundational to the study of Romans from here on out (2004; 2011; 2016; 2024).

Each of these readings has merit, but they share a limitation. What they overlook is the deeper mythic imagination that saturates Paul's thought. Paul was a Jew of the eastern Mediterranean—a world still haunted by Babylonian, Canaanite, and Hellenistic myths of divine embodiment and monstrous opposition (Putthoff, 2017; 2020). After his Damascus experience, Paul withdrew not to Athens or Rome but to Syria and Arabia (Galatians 1:17), which was territory still breathing with the old cosmologies that echoed the mythic imagination of the ancient Near East (cf. Flusser, 1988; Safrai, 1976; Weinfeld, 1983). There, I suspect, Paul steeped himself in the stories, languages, and symbols of that older world, the very currents that later surface in his letters as the mythic grammar of Sin, Death, and Spirit. In that environment, the idea that a spirit could inhabit a person's body, or that the old Canaanite and Israelite ideas of Sin and Death, were far less metaphorical than they were ontological.

To bring Paul back into that world is to see that his language of Sin dwelling in me (7:17, 20) and Death reigning (5:14, 17) is not rhetorical flourish. It is theological realism. In his imagination, as we'll see, Sin and Death are rogue divinities—fallen cosmic agents—that exploit the human vessel the way parasites exploit a host (Gaventa, 2024; Käsemann, 1994). They are not created evils, but divine perversions: entities with will, appetite, and domain.

This understanding also explains the sharp transition between Romans 7 and 8. The same verb Paul uses to describe Sin's indwelling (*oikei*, "it dwells in me," 7:17) he uses again for the Spirit in 8:9–11 ("the Spirit of God dwells [*oikei*] in you"). The shift is ontological: the tenant changes, and the haunted house becomes a temple again.

And this is the heart of Paul's anthropology. Humans are not self-contained moral agents choosing between good and evil. We are hybrid beings—earth and breath, dust and spirit (Genesis 2:7)—designed to be indwelt. Our problem is not that we do wrong; it's that the wrong power lives in us. And salvation, for Paul, is not primarily pardon or reform but repossession (Schweitzer, 1931).

Romans 7 is therefore neither psychology nor metaphor alone. It is possession theology—an anatomy of haunted embodiment. And to grasp its depth, we must read it as Paul intended: as an account of the monstrous within, where Sin and Death take up residence in the house of the human self.

## SIN, DEATH, AND THE DISORDERING OF CREATION (ROMANS 5–6)

Before Paul ever cries out, "Who will rescue me from this body of Death?" in Romans 7, he has already told the story of how the monsters got in. Romans 5–6 is the prequel—the invasion narrative—the moment the boundaries of creation were breached and Sin and Death crossed the threshold of the world.

Paul opens his account with one of the most compressed and explosive sentences in the New Testament:

> Just as through one human Sin entered the world, and through Sin, Death... (*hōsper dia henos anthrōpou hē hamartia eis ton kosmon eisēlthen, kai dia tēs hamartias ho thanatos...*, Romans 5:12).

Two prepositions do all the mythic heavy lifting: *dia* ("through") and *eis* ("into"). They are spatial terms, tunnel terms, breach terms. Paul is not saying, "Because Adam sinned, we feel guilty," or "Adam gave us a bad example," or some ambiguous notion about "original sin" or "sin nature." He is describing an incursion. Sin entered into the world, and Death entered through Sin. Adam, in Paul's imagination, functions like a cosmic doorway—the portal through which two hostile powers infiltrated created space (Wright, 2013).

Paul's ancient audience would not have heard abstraction. They knew the old stories: chaos beings slipping over boundaries, Mōt crossing from the underworld into the land of the living, Tiamat's brood flooding the ordered cosmos, the Rabisu demons of Mesopotamia entering homes when a threshold was left unguarded. Paul is not copying these myths, but he is working within the same intellectual grammar—the grammar of ontological invasion. What Israel called Sin and Death, the ancient Near East imagined in other monstrous forms. Either way, the world becomes haunted because something foreign has entered it.

Paul's language in Romans 5:12–21 pushes this even further. Adam is not simply a sinner; he is a place, a spatiotemporal field, the zone in which humanity now exists. When he says we are "in Adam," he means it literally—the way one lives in a city or in a climate. Adam is the realm governed by corruption and decay (Hooker, 1990; Jewett, 2007; Moo, 2018). The Adam-event fractures creation's boundary, and through that breach, Sin and Death establish a regime.

This is why Paul can speak in both directions:

- We live "in Sin" (*tē hamartia*, Romans 6:2).
- Sin lives "in us" (*oikousa en emoi hē hamartia*, Romans 7:17, cf. v. 20).

It is a mutual indwelling—a symbiosis gone wrong (cf. Gaventa, 2024). Humanity is not merely morally compromised; humanity is inhabited. The monstrous powers do not merely influence us; they occupy us.

Adam becomes the original host. What begins with him becomes the condition of all who share his flesh.

Paul's temporal imagination matches his spatial imagination. Once the incursion occurs, he says, "Death reigned" (*ho thanatos ebasileusen*, Romans 5:14, 17). The verb *ebasileusen* ("reigned") is political language (Käsemann, 1971; Wright, 2013). Death has established a kingdom. Time itself bends under the weight of this power. Human existence becomes a long march toward dissolution because the timeline humanity occupies is itself corrupted. The spatiotemporal environment of Adam guarantees decay. In Jewish thought, the human self is mimetic—it reflects the nature of the space it inhabits (Putthoff, 2017). Life in fallen space means sharing in its falling. Life in dying space means sharing in its death.

Adam, then, is not simply the first sinner. He is the cosmic architecture within which all human life takes place—the haunted house at the scale of the world (cf. Putthoff, 2017).

But Paul insists that another architecture has been established. If Adam is a space, Christ is also a space. If Adam is the realm of invasion, Christ is the realm of restoration (Schweitzer, 1931).

> Much more will those who receive the abundance of grace... reign in life through the one, Jesus Christ (*dia tou henos Iēsou Christou*, Romans 5:17).

Paul's contrast between Adam and Christ is not moral but ontological. Two zones, two powers, two worlds. One leads toward Death, and the other toward Life (Schweitzer, 1931).

This is why Paul assumes the Romans already know the meaning of baptism:

> Do you not know that all of us who were baptized into Christ Jesus were baptized into his death? (*hē agnoiēte hoti hosoi ebaptisthēmen eis Christon Iēsoun eis ton thanaton autou ebaptisthēmen*, Romans 6:3)

Baptism is not a ritual wash. It is a migration. A border crossing. A transfer of citizenship from one cosmic domain to another (Wright, 2013; Campbell, 2009). Baptism joins us to Christ's death, he says, so that we may "walk in newness of life" (Romans 6:4). Paul's verbs are spatial again, as we are buried with him, united with him, freed from Sin, and released to "walk" in a new terrain. Romans 6 is not about moral improvement (Schweitzer, 1931). It is about changing one's cosmic address.

This sets up everything Paul is about to say in Romans 7. The human condition is not primarily a psychological battle between conscience and desire. It is a territorial conflict—a battle over who occupies the house of the self. Adam's breach allowed Sin and Death to take up residence. Christ's death and resurrection open a door into a new realm. Romans 5–6 tell the story of how the monsters entered. Romans 7 tells the story of what they do once inside.

## SIN'S AWAKENING THROUGH THE LAW (ROMANS 7:7–13)

Paul's initial thoughts on the state of the human self are nothing short of the cries of a haunted man:

> What then shall we say? Is the Law Sin (*ho nomos hamartia*)? By no means! Yet if it had not been for the Law, I would not have known Sin (*ouk egnōn tēn hamartian*). For I would not have known what it is to desire (*epithymian*) if the Law had not said, "You shall not covet." But Sin (*hē hamartia*), seizing an opportunity (*aphormēn de lambousa*) through the commandment (*dia tēs entolēs*), produced in me (*kateirgasato en emoi*) all kinds of desire (*pasan epithymian*). Apart from the Law, Sin is dead (*hamartia nekra*, Romans 7:7–8).

Paul begins this section with the most radical question imaginable to a Jewish audience: "Is the Law Sin?" That is, could the Torah—the sacred revelation of God—be in some way complicit in evil? His answer, immediately emphatic, is *mē genoito!* ("By no means!"), the strongest Greek negation possible. And yet his logic will be far less reassuring than his opening denial.

Paul's claim is not that the Law is evil, but that it has become a host—a site that Sin can occupy. His grammar gives the whole argument its shape: Sin, taking an opportunity (*aphormē*) through the commandment, produced in me all manner of desire (*epithymia*, v. 8). The key word here, *aphormē*, was a military term. It literally meant a base of operations—the forward staging ground from which a campaign was launched (cf. Wasserman, 2008; Dunn, 1988; Käsemann, 1994). Greek historians used it this way: Thucydides describes the Peloponnese as an *aphormē*—a secure base and point of withdrawal for the Peloponnesians (*Thuc.*, 1.90). Xenophon likewise speaks of establishing an *aphormē* in military situations as the tactical first move in securing a region (Xenophon, *Anabasis* 4.3.31). In Roman military strategy, an *aphormē* was like the beachhead, the fortified point where an invading army gained access to enemy territory. In military contexts, the term denotes a secure foothold or staging point—a location that enables movement, supply, and coordinated action rather than mere opportunity or occasion.

For Paul, that beachhead is the Torah itself.

This is an extraordinary reimagining of Israel's sacred text. In Jewish tradition, Torah was the bulwark against evil—the means by which Israel resisted idolatry and impurity. But in Paul's telling, it becomes the point of entry. Sin is not destroyed by contact with the Law. It is instead awakened. The commandment itself becomes the doorway through which the invader crosses the threshold.

This paradox is deeply rooted in the Bible's own narrative. The Law, after all, is the divine word spoken into human history—and in the biblical imagination, divine speech has creative power. In Genesis 1, God's words call the world into being. In Mesopotamian tradition, the gods' creative decrees are inscribed on the *Mē* tablets, the cosmic blueprints that sustain and regulate the universe (as described in *Enki and the World Order*). But in the Babylonian *Enuma Elish*, that same divine speech becomes a medium of rebellion when Tiamat, the primordial sea goddess, utters her own counter-creation, summoning the *ummaṭū*—a brood of monstrous hybrids who embody her chaos (Tablet I). Paul's point echoes that ancient anxiety: the word that gives life can also, when twisted, become a channel for chaos. Sin does not create, but it corrupts creation's language.

Paul illustrates this with the example of coveting: "I would not have known desire (*epithymia*) if the Law had not said, 'You shall not covet.'" He quotes from the Tenth Commandment (Exodus 20:17; Deuteronomy 5:21 LXX), which forbids not an outward act but an inward state of desire. In that subtle move—from action to intention—Paul finds the commandment's vulnerability. The moment the Law enters the heart, Sin finds its foothold. What was meant to curb desire instead stirs it.

The term *epithymia* ("desire, craving") has a rich life both in Scripture and in philosophy. In Greek moral discourse, it often described unruly desires opposing reason, conditions the Stoics treated therapeutically, as Epictetus explains when he compares unchecked desire to illness requiring prompt rational treatment before it hardens and reasserts itself again (*Disc.* 2.26). In the Hebrew Bible, the corresponding concept, *ta'avah*, is more than appetite; it is spiritual distortion—Israel "craved intensely" in the wilderness, a yearning that led them toward idolatrous rebellion (Numbers 11:4), and the psalmist reflects that they "lusted exceedingly in the desert" (Psalm 106:14). Paul merges both senses. Desire becomes not merely human weakness but spiritual infection—a symptom of Sin's presence within.

Then comes one of the more startling lines: "Apart from the Law, Sin is dead" (*chōris nomou hamartia nekra*, Romans 7:8). The statement drips with irony. One might expect the Law to *kill* Sin. Instead, the Law is what gives Sin *life*. Without a divine word to twist, Sin lies dormant, but when the commandment arrives, it wakes like a creature roused from sleep.

A striking textual variant in Romans 7:8 sharpens Paul's imagery. The main text reads "Sin is dead" (*hamartia nekra*), but some manuscripts expand this into "Sin *was* dead" (*hamartia nekra ēn* [F G latt syᵖ bo]/*ēn nekra* [K]). These expansions reflect what Paul's syntax already implies: before the commandment arrived, Sin existed as a dormant power—lifeless, inert, unincarnate. In other words, Paul is not denying Sin's existence prior to the law, but he is portraying it as a latent power that only becomes active, embodied, and lethal once the commandment provides it a point of entry.

Only when the commandment comes does Sin "revive" (*anezēsen*, Romans 7:9) and enter into active possession of the human body. Paul's language therefore treats Sin not as moral failure but as a monster with a life-cycle: dead, revived, indwelling, and finally condemned in Christ's flesh (8:3). We'll deal with this more fully in a moment.

Paul uses the verb *anezēsen*—"came to life again"—to describe this reanimation. The term comes from *anazaō*, meaning "to revive" or "to come back to life," and in the LXX it usually describes resurrection or restoration. In narrative contexts, the verb can mark a return to active vitality after apparent cessation. In Paul's hands, the verb is grotesquely inverted. Sin, not the righteous, is resurrected. What should remain dead revives. The word that once raised the dead (in the prophets) now resuscitates Sin itself.

This is Paul's theology of the undead. Sin, in his imagination, is not static or abstract—it is animate and cyclical, like the god Mōt in the Ugaritic *Baal Cycle*. As we saw above, in that myth, Mōt ("Death") devours the storm god Baal, descends to the underworld, and is later resurrected, rising again to devour anew. Paul's "Sin revived" (*hē hamartia anezēsen*, Romans 7:9) plays in the same register: a monstrous being, always killed but never gone, roused to fresh hunger each time the Law is proclaimed.

When he adds, "then I died" (*egō de apethanon*, 7:9), the effect is devastating. Meant to give life, the Law in fact becomes the weapon of Death. Paul's phrase, Sin "deceived me and killed (me)" (*exēpatēsen me kai dia autes apekteinen*, v. 11), draws quite explicitly on Genesis 3. The Greek verb *exēpatēsen* ("deceived") is quite close to Eve's confession in the LXX: "The serpent deceived me"—*ho ophis ēpatēsen me* (Genesis

3:13 LXX). Paul is not making an incidental echo. He is rewriting Eden as anthropology (Gaventa, 2004). The serpent of Genesis—the deceiver who twists God's command—is now internalized as a force within the self. Sin is not the serpent but more like the serpent's heir. Its medium is the commandment, and its prey is the human will.

The next clause—"through it [the commandment], it [Sin] killed me" (*dia autēs apekteinen*)—has a textual nuance worth noting. The verb *apokteinō* connotes deliberate killing, often with ritual or violent overtones. In the Septuagint, it is used for Cain's premeditated slaying of Abel (Genesis 4:8 LXX) and for the judicial execution of the prophets (1 Kings 18:13 LXX). Greek writers likewise employ *apokteinō* for intentional, agent-driven violence, as when Aeschylus describes Xerxes warriors' plan to "slaughter" their Hellenic enemies in battle (*Pers.* 452). The force of Paul's wording is unmistakable: Sin acts with will, strategy, and lethal intent. It is not passive rebellion but active predator.

Here again, the echoes multiply. In Genesis 4, God warns Cain that "Sin is crouching at the door. Its desire is for you, but you must master it" (*pros se hē apostrophē autou, kai su arxeis autou*, Genesis 4:7 LXX). The LXX's *apostrophē*—"turning," "orientation toward"—depicts Sin as a power facing Cain, poised in relational proximity, a nuance often used in ancient sources of hostile forces aligning themselves toward a target or object. In the Genesis scene, Sin is the beast at the threshold, coiled and waiting for the moment of passage. Paul's phrase "through the commandment" (*dia tēs entolēs*) mirrors this threshold imagery. The commandment becomes the doorway, the Law the opened entrance, and Sin—like the crouching predator—springs across the threshold into its host.

Ancient Jewish wisdom literature already wrestled with this paradox. *Wisdom of Solomon* 2:24 blames "the envy of the devil" for Death's intrusion into the world. *Sirach* 15:11–20 warns, "Do not say, 'It was through the Lord I fell away'… He has placed before you fire and water; stretch out your hand to whichever you choose." Paul fuses both traditions. Sin enters through divine command, but its agency is entirely its own. The Law is good, and the invader is evil, but when the two become entangled, humanity is caught in the crossfire.

Romans 7:12 crystallizes Paul's tension: "So then, the Law is holy, and the commandment is holy and righteous and good." The Law's goodness is not revoked—but its goodness now serves to expose Sin's monstrosity. The syntax of verse 13 is revealing, as Paul adds: *hina phanē hamartia*—"so that Sin might appear as Sin." The purpose of the Law, paradoxically, is not to make humans good but to unmask the invader. It is to allow Sin in so that it can reveal Sin for what Sin really is.

This verb *phanē* ("to appear") carries the sense of revelation or manifestation—it's the same root used for epiphany (*epiphaneia*), an appearance of a god, the term used in Greek inscriptions and literature to describe divine visitations, such as Apollo's "epiphany" at Delphi (Pausanias, *Descr.* 10.24.6) or Athena's sudden manifestation in Homer (*Od.* 13.221). What Paul suggests, with almost mythic irony, is that the Law functions as a kind of theophany—a manifestation not of God, but of Sin. The holy commandment becomes the stage on which Sin reveals itself for what it really is: a power pretending to divinity, revealed in its ugliness when it dares to speak through the word of God.

The Hebrew Scriptures had already personified Death (*māwet*) in similar terms. In Job 18:13–14, "the firstborn of Death" (*bekor māwet*) devours his limbs (*yōʾkhal baddāyw*), and the victim is "torn" (*yinnāteq*: "pulled up, uprooted") from the tent of his trust and marched before the king of terrors (*melekh baʿalōt*). Sin's exposure, for Paul, is like that— the unveiling of a hidden monarch who rules unseen. In Rabbinic tradition, the same logic unfolds: "One sin leads to another" (*Avot* 4:2). Sin behaves not merely as an act but as an agent—a self-perpetuating force, reproductive, alive.

The sequence of Romans 7:7–13 thus forms a grim parody of creation. The divine word speaks, and a new being arises. But instead of light, there is darkness. Instead of order, disorder. Instead of the Spirit animating clay, Sin animates the flesh. The Law does not cause this—it reveals it. So the problem is not Torah but tenancy. The holy word, entering human hearing, finds that another voice is already speaking inside.

In Paul's world, this is not metaphor. It is spiritual realism. To be human is to be a vessel, but the question is always: who lives here? And if it is Sin inside, as Paul clearly believes to be the case, then how can it be expelled, its power nullified? Unfortunately, the Law alone cannot cleanse the house. It can only expose the squatter, shine light on its horrific essence, and call it out as the unlawful ruler that it is. The commandment illuminates the room—and what's revealed inside is a monster.

## THE DIVIDED AND POSSESSED SELF (ROMANS 7:14–20)

Paul continues in the next segment by expanding on the nature of and interactions between Law, Sin, and the self. As he writes:

For we know that the Law is spiritual (*ho nomos pneumatikos estin*), but I am fleshly (*sarkinos*), sold under Sin (*pepramenos hypo tēn hamartian*). For I do not understand (*ou ginōskō*) my own actions. For I do not do (*ou gar ho thelō touto prassō*) what I want, but I do the very thing I hate (*ho misō touto poiō*). Now if I do what I do not want, I agree with the Law that it is good. So now it is no longer I who do it, but Sin dwelling in me (*hē oikousa en emoi hamartia*)— for I know that nothing good dwells in me (*ouk oikei en emoi … agathon*), that is, in my flesh (*en tē sarki mou*). For the desire is present (*to gar thelein parakeitai*), but the ability to carry it out is not good (*to de katergazesthai to kalon ou*, Romans 7:14–20).

## "I am fleshly, sold under Sin" (v. 14)

Paul's diagnosis of the human condition begins with a jarring confession: "I am *sarkinos*, sold under Sin." The adjective *sarkinos* literally means "fleshly" or "made of flesh," not simply "sinful," as so many traditions have wrongly assumed. The nuance is critically important. *Sarx* in Paul does not refer to skin or muscle, but to the entire human condition when severed from divine Spirit (*pneuma*). The Law, he says, is *pneumatikos*—spiritual, emanating from God's own essence and life. By contrast, the human being is *sarkinos*—fleshly, a creature whose material composition renders it vulnerable, porous, and susceptible to outside influence. Flesh is not evil, but it is permeable and thus vulnerable to evil influencers.

The second phrase, *pepramenos hypo tēn hamartian* ("sold under Sin"), comes from the world of slavery and commerce. The verb *pipraskō* means "to sell," most often the selling of a person into servitude. Thus, the LXX uses the verb in Isaiah 50:1 for God "selling" his people because of their sins. The idiom "sold under Sin" echoes Israel's own laments about bondage: Elijah rebukes Ahab, "You have sold yourself" (*ta pepērakos*, 1 Kings 21:20 LXX) to do what is evil in the sight of the LORD. Paul repurposes that imagery from national apostasy to individual anthropology. The self is a trafficked body, a commodity placed on the auction block of Sin (Käsemann, 1969; Segal, 1990; Barclay, 2015).

This imagery has deep roots in Jewish apocalyptic thought. The *Community Rule* from Qumran speaks of humanity as divided between "the spirit of truth and the spirit of perversity" (1QS 3–4). Each human life, it says, is governed by one or the other—no one is neutral. Paul's language belongs to that same world. "Sold under Sin" is not mere moral hyperbole—it is covenantal slavery. In the Second Temple Jewish imagination, to be ruled by the wrong spirit was to be owned by it, to be enrolled in the lot of Belial rather than the lot of God. The flesh, lacking the indwelling Spirit, becomes contested space—a jurisdiction where the "spirit of perversity" exercises legal authority. Paul's phrase "sold under Sin" (*pepramenos hypo tēn hamartian*) identifies the self as one transferred into the wrong dominion, a captive whose body now falls under the administration of an alien power. And in the next lines, Paul shows what that slavery looks like from the inside: the will overrun, the mind divided, the limbs commanded by a force too powerful for the self to resist on its own.

## Conflicted Agency (vv. 15–17)

Paul's next lines spiral into syntactic confusion, mirroring the chaos he describes:

> For what I do (*ho gar katergazomai*) I do not understand (*ou ginōskō*); for what I want I do not do (*ou gar ho thelō touto prassō*), but what I hate (*ho misō*)—this I practice (*touto poiō*). ... So now it is no longer I who do it, but Sin dwelling in me (*alla hē oikousa en emoi hamartia*, Romans 7:15–17).

The chain of negations—*ou*, *ouk*, *ouketi*—creates a sort of rhythmic disorientation. The Greek clauses trip over one another as if the syntax itself were possessed. It is one of the rare cases where Paul's grammar performs his theology. It's as if his emotions overwhelm him and derail his attempt at maintaining a logical demeanor. Ancient rhetoricians even noted that such piling negations could mimic mental fracture or agitation, the kind of speech one produces when overtaken by something stronger than oneself. Paul's syntax stumbles forward, doubling back, contradicting itself. The structure enacts the breakdown of agency: the "I" quite literally loses coherence.

The crucial verb reappears in v. 17: "It is no longer I who do it, but Sin dwelling (*oikousa*) in me." The participle *oikousa* (from *oikeō*, "to dwell, reside") belongs to the vocabulary of habitation. In ordinary Greek, it could describe a person living in a house—or a deity's temple, as when Herodotus speaks of the refusal to submit to Xerxes for destroying the gods' "houses" (*Hist.*, 8.143), or when the Egyptian sources that call the deity's temple a "house" (*P. Oxy.*, 11.1380.2). Paul's choice of this term is deliberate and real. The human body is the house—or the temple (1 Corinthians 3:16)—and the usurper has moved in. He'll use the same verb later to describe the Spirit's indwelling (Romans 8:9–11)—a calculated symmetry that frames salvation as an eviction and replacement of tenants.

This "inhabiting Sin" recalls the ancient imagery of God's divine glory dwelling in the sanctuary (Exodus 25:8). What Paul describes is a false indwelling that mimics divine presence but desecrates the space. The human temple has been turned into a house of another god.

The Jewish philosopher Philo, roughly Paul's contemporary, uses similar imagery when he describes the passions as in need of discipline (*Agr.*, 158). For Philo, these tenants can be disciplined and expelled through the cultivation of reason (*logos*), which restores harmony to the inner life. Paul radicalizes the metaphor. The problem, for him, is not merely unruly emotions but an invading sovereignty. Reason itself has been commandeered. The "I" does not simply lose control of its passions—it loses control of its agency. Where Philo believes moral purification can reclaim the house, Paul insists the house has been overtaken by a power against which reason is helpless until a stronger indweller arrives.

Ancient Near Eastern texts illuminate how literal this language would have sounded to Paul's audience. The Mesopotamian *Maqlū* ("Burning") incantation series, used in exorcism rituals, describes spirits and forces that enter the body of the victim, dwell in their flesh, and seemingly take command of their limbs (*Maqlū* I–II). The afflicted speaker in these tablets often shifts between first-person narration and attributing his actions to the invading force—precisely the dynamic Paul articulates in Romans 7. Paul's "I do not understand what I do" would have resonated uncannily with such laments. In the ancient worldview, possession was not fantasy but a recognized category of experience: when one's body acted against one's will, it was because another will had moved in.

Modern readers may reach for psychological language—split personality, addiction, compulsion—but Paul's world had no such frameworks. He describes a theological anthropology where the human being is a vessel designed for occupancy. As I argued elsewhere (Putthoff 2017; 2020), ancient Jewish and Near Eastern anthropology consistently pictured the self as space—an architectural locus where divine breath or rival powers could dwell. Paul stands firmly within that lineage, describing the dark impacts of the experience of embodiment.

### *"Nothing good dwells in me" (vv. 18–20)*

The next remarks deepen the paradox:

For I know that nothing good dwells in me (*ouk oikei en emoi ... agathon*), that is, in my flesh (*en tē sarki mou*). For to will (*to gar thelein*) is present with me (*parakeitai moi*), but to work it out (*to de katergazesthai*) is not. For I do not do the good I want (*ou gar ho thelō poiō agathon*), but the evil I do not want (*ho ou thelō kakon*)—this I practice (*touto prassō*). Now if I do what I do not want (*ei de ho ou thelō touto ... poiō*), it is no longer I who do it (*ouketi egō katergazomai*), but Sin dwelling in me (*alla hē oikousa en emoi hamartia*, Romans 7:18–20).

The repetition of *oikei* ("dwells") underscores that Paul is still speaking of tenancy, not temperament. The problem is not that flesh is intrinsically corrupt. This is not the later Western doctrine of original sin—the idea that all humans inherit Adam's guilt—or the popular evangelical notion of a permanent "sin nature" lodged inside the self. Paul's point is far stranger and far more concrete: the occupant within the flesh is corrupt. In other words, the body is sacred architecture occupied by a blasphemous tenant. The dilemma is not that humans are depraved, but that humans are invaded.

Paul's syntax mimics the tug-of-war: "the willing is present with me, but the doing of the good I do not find" (*to gar thelein parakeitai moi, to de katergazesthai to kalon ou*, v. 18). The juxtaposition of *thelein* ("to will") and *katergazesthai* ("to carry out") captures the collapse between intention and action. The participial rhythm conveys a kind of spiritual arrhythmia—the inner pulse out of sync with the body's movement. Ancient writers used similar language to describe bodies overridden by another force. In the *Maqlū* incantations, the sufferer laments that inner intention seeks one thing, while their actions follow another force (*Maqlū* II). The urgency of the situation is such that extreme actions must be taken and rituals enacted in order to remedy the condition. Paul taps into that same experiential grammar. His Greek does not merely describe conflict. It performs it, the will leaning forward while the deed staggers behind, revealing a self divided by competing indwellers.

This description of the human condition echoes prophetic visions of desecrated space. In Ezekiel 8–11, the prophet sees the Glory of YHWH depart from the temple, leaving behind abominations—idols, creeping things, human remains—filling the void where holiness once dwelled. Only after that withdrawal can judgment, cleansing, and eventual restoration unfold. Paul's anthropology follows the same theological sequence: the divine Glory has seemingly departed, the vacancy has been exploited, and the rival power has taken possession.

Sin is not simply active—it is enthroned. The human self has become the abandoned sanctuary Ezekiel saw. As we'll see, Romans 8 narrates the reversal of that catastrophe: the return of the divine presence, when "the Spirit of him who raised Jesus from the dead dwells (*oikei*) in you" (Romans 8:11).

Paul's theology of Sin's indwelling and the Spirit's counter-indwelling therefore hinge on the same verb. The correspondence is a deliberate polemic. The human body, once God's home, has been leased to a squatter. Redemption is the legal eviction of that tenant and the re-enthronement of the rightful owner.

The result is the most harrowing picture of the human self in Scripture: an "I" at war with itself. "I do not do the good I want, but the evil I do not want is what I do" (*ou gar ho thelō poiō agathon, alla ho ou thelō kakon touto prassō*, Romans 7:19). The line reverberates with the pathos of captivity. These verbs—*thelō* ("I want"), *poieō* ("I do"), *prassō* ("I practice")—are not metaphors for mood or personality, nor even descriptions of ordinary human inconsistency. They depict coercion. The body behaves as though it is under foreign command *because it is*. Paul is not lamenting moral weakness. He is instead describing his own self commandeered by another will, an embodied creature whose limbs obey the occupying force that has seized the house.

Behind the lament stands the shadow of ancient myth. Ugaritic poetry depicts the god Mōt as boasting of his limitless appetite, consuming gods and mortals alike without ever being satisfied (KTU 1.5; cf. 1.6). Mōt is not simply death-as-event but Death-as-devourer—the insatiable mouth that consumes gods and humans without distinction. To be "sold under Sin" is to host that hunger within. The devourer's throne, however, is not *out there* somewhere, threatening human existence from without. It is inside the human self, seeking to consume from within, turning the body into the chamber where the ancient eater feeds.

For Paul, then, Romans 7:14–20 is not a moral struggle between reason and desire—it is a possession narrative. Flesh is not simply weak. It is inhabited. And the Law, though spiritual, cannot evict the intruder. The self can recognize the goodness of the Law but lacks the agency to perform it. Only an outside power can reclaim the house. The tragedy of Romans 7 is that the voice crying "I" is no longer its own master—it is enslaved to Sin. The miracle of Romans 8 will be that the same house still stands—but the true Lord intends to move back in.

## THE LAW IN MY MEMBERS (ROMANS 7:21–23)

The self is the site of a battle between good and evil, between the forces of God and Sin:

> So I find this law at work (*heuriskō ara ton nomon*): when I want to do what is good (*tō thelonti emoi poiein to kalon*), evil lies beside me (*kakon parakeitai moi*). For I delight in the Law of God (*synēdomai gar tō nomō tou theou*) in my inner being (*kata ton esō anthrōpon*), but I see another law (*heteron nomon*) in my members (*en tois melesin mou*) waging war (*antistrateuomenon*) against the law of my mind (*tō nomō tou noos mou*) and making me captive (*aichmalōtizonta me*) to the Law of Sin (*tō nomō tēs hamartias*) that exists in my members (*tō onti en tois melesin mou*, Romans 7:21–23).

Paul's tone here is precise. But it is the tone of a weary man. The verbs shift from heart felt confession to more of an observation, as though he is cataloguing symptoms of an inner occupation. Verse 21 opens with the chilling line: "When I want to do good, evil lies beside me."

The key phrase, to *kakon parakeitai*, literally means "lies beside" or "is laid down next to." It evokes not moral proximity but spatial intimacy—the way a thing is placed flush against another. It is used for circumstances side by side (*parakeimai*) in Plato (*Phileb.* 24d) or of the way bodies lie next to each other in Homeric scenes of sleep (*Od.* 14.521). The term can denote physical closeness so immediate that the two things share the same space without blending. Paul could have said "evil is *within* me" (*en emoi*), but instead he says "it lies beside me." The distinction is subtle but unnerving. Sin is not simply internal. It is adjacent, a constant companion, a shadow that refuses to detach. Evil is therefore not merely present in the world—it is on the bed next to Paul.

This line unmistakably echoes Genesis 4:7, where God warns Cain, "Sin is crouching at your door. Its desire is for you, but you must master it." The Greek of the Septuagint literally renders the original Hebrew as, "Its turning is toward you" (*pros se hē apistrophē autou*). That is, Sin faces you, watching, waiting. Paul recasts that image of the crouching beast as a constant companion. The predator is no longer outside lying in wait at the door. It has moved indoors. Evil now "lies beside" the self, sharing the same space, breathing the same air. The psychological and spatial boundaries have collapsed. What Genesis pictured as a threshold threat has become, in Paul, an invasive roommate—an unwelcome presence occupying the same room, leaning over the same table, murmuring in the same ear.

In modern language, we might call this codependence or internal conflict, as in Epictetus's description of the divided self (*Ench.* 2), but in Paul's cosmology it is ontological proximity—two presences sharing one house. In Aeschylus's *Agamemnon*, Clytemnestra portrays the Erinyes as relentless avenging powers that cling intimately and invisibly to human life (*Ag.* 1185–1190), a chilling parallel to Paul's vision of evil as an intimate presence. Evil is no longer the distant threat of the serpent or the beast of Sheol. It is a neighbor lodged too near, whispering over the fence of the flesh, waiting for the perfect moment to impose its will onto the human self.

### The War of Laws (vv. 22–23)

Paul deepens the image with a pair of opposing laws: *nomos tou noos* ("law of the mind") versus *nomos tēs hamartias* ("law of Sin"). The word *nomos* here does not mean "legal code," as so many interpreters have assumed. Philo uses *nomos* of the law of nature (*Abr.* 135) or the human embodiment of the law (*Vit. Mos.* 1.162). It is not about a set of writings external to the self that provide guidelines for how humans should live. Instead, it denotes a principle or operating power that governs behavior—an internalized regimen, the ruling logic of a system. Paul sees two such laws installed in the same person: one delights in the divine order (*nomos tou theou*, v. 22), while the other issues commands "in my members" (*en tois melesin mou*, v. 23). This phrase is used elsewhere to describe passions waging war within the body.

Some manuscripts heighten the imagery by duplicating the phrase "in my members" (*en tois melesin mou*), thereby stressing the bodily localization of the struggle (for example, a double reading preserved in multiple Western witnesses, including D and several Old Latin manuscripts). Whether original to Paul or a later scribal expansion, the repetition makes the point clearly: this is not a contest of ideas or written norms, but of limbs governed by two rival operating systems at once. The human body itself has become the war zone, the site of *Chaoskampf* (Stowers, 1994; Wasserman, 2008; Davies, 2022). The language of war is explicit as well. As Paul insists, "I see another law in my members waging war (*antistrateuomenon*) against the law of my mind" (Romans 7:23). The verb *antistrateuomai* is military, meaning to lead an assault or wage a campaign against an enemy. In other Greek texts, the term appears in overtly martial settings, describing organized assaults and counter-moves—language drawn from real campaigns rather than metaphorical debates. Paul imagines the interior of the human self as a battlefield—a miniature cosmos in which rival powers clash for dominion.

This is not a new metaphor in Jewish thought. In *4 Ezra* 7:92, the seer laments that the evil heart has grown within and has led humans astray toward death. The same internalized warfare appears in the Dead Sea Scrolls from Qumran, where the author(s) speak of the spirits of truth struggling against the spirits of deceit (1QS 3.18–19). In the *Community Rule*, the writer describes these spirits and humanity as being ensnared in a battle between good and evil, depicting an inner conflict that mirrors the external cosmic struggle (1QS 3.18–26). For Paul, this language now crystallizes into a single drama: the human being is the terrain of the cosmic war.

Greco-Roman philosophy offers an illuminating contrast. In Plato's *Republic* (4.439d–441c), Socrates describes the tripartite soul—three faculties locked in constant tension. These are "reason" (*logos*), "spirit" (*thymos*), and "appetite" (*epithymia*), and human flourishing—or "virtue" (*aretē*)—is the harmony produced when the *logos* governs the other two. At first glance, Paul's struggle sounds superficially similar, but the engine is entirely different. The conflict in Romans 7 is not between parts of the psyche but between powers that have taken up residence within the boundaries of the self. Paul's "law of Sin" is not the irrational part of the soul—it is a rival sovereignty. Likewise, the "law of the mind" is not philosophical intellect—it is the sphere where the Spirit's influence is meant to reign. The opposition is thus spiritual, not merely psychological. It is not, in other words, that Paul is torn because he himself cannot make the right decision. It's because the apparatus by which he would otherwise be able to behave rightly has been hijacked by a force whose aim is to cause disorder through its new host body. It is a conflict between two indwellers, two legal orders, contending for possession of the same flesh.

This imagery recalls the cosmic wars of the ancient Near East, but Paul relocates them within the human frame. In the *Baal Cycle* from Ugarit, the storm-god Baal battles Mōt, the god of Death, for control of the world's fertility. Their struggle tears creation apart: Baal descends into Mōt's maw, Mōt bursts forth again from the earth, and order and chaos alternate in endless cycle. Paul internalizes that mythic oscillation. The war between Baal and Mōt, between life and Death, now takes place not in the heavens or the soil but in the body. "I see another law in my members," he says. The human being has become the new cosmos—the self-sized battlefield where the old gods still fight.

In Paul's thought, the "members" (*melē*) of the body are not morally neutral. Each limb is an "instrument" (*hoplon*, Romans 6:13) that can be enlisted either for righteousness or for Sin. Paul envisions these as conscripted soldiers. The mind—the seat of desire for God's law—issues commands, but another law intercepts them, rerouting the limbs to obey a different master. The result is paralysis.

Notice how personal the language remains. The "law of the mind" is not abstract principle but a *nomos* that "delights in the law of God" (v. 22). The inner self still recognizes the good—Paul still knows what's right and wrong and how he should behave. But the tragedy is that its recognition does not translate into action. His will to obey is present, but his command of his own body has been lost. The occupying force issues counter-orders that he cannot disobey, even if he wants to.

This interior *Chaoskampf*—the battle between divine order and chaos—has been brought down to the scale of the flesh. The human body becomes the new world-body, its inner geography echoing the cosmos itself. The battle that has long been raging between good and evil in the heavenly and earthly realms has now found its way into the boundaries of the human self. Here, the mind corresponds to heaven and the members to earth, and Sin moves like an underworld god beneath the surface, rising up to claim dominion. The ancient cosmic drama—once depicted in epic tales of battles between the storm and the sea, between dragons and deities—now takes place within the space of Paul's own body.

The Law of God remains holy, but Paul's lament reveals its impotence. Torah can identify the enemy, but it cannot dislodge it. The "law of the mind" desires obedience but lacks dominion. The Law is a map of order given to a world already occupied by chaos.

Thus, by verse 23, the human being is not a sinner wrestling with temptation but a captive soldier in a cosmic war. The verbs begin to pile up: *blepō* ("I see"), *antistrateuomenon* ("waging war"), *aichmalōtizonta* ("taking captive"). The last term, *aichmalōtizō*, was used for prisoners of war—those seized and marched off by a victorious army, as in Diodorus Siculus likewise uses the language of wartime captivity to describe defeated enemies seized and carried off as prisoners following armed conflict (*Diod.* 14.37). Josephus likewise depicts wartime subjugation in explicitly corporeal terms, describing populations seized, slaughtered, and carried off into captivity following Roman conquest (*BJ* 4.8.1). Paul's imagery is quite clear: the body is the battlefield, the will is the besieged city, and Sin has taken hostages who now await liberation by their Savior.

## The Cry for Deliverance (vv. 24–25)

After tracing the descent of Sin into the very limbs of the body, Paul's argument reaches its breaking point. The syntax itself seems to collapse under the weight of the tension. Verse 24 erupts not in reasoned theology but in a liturgical cry:

> Wretched man that I am! Who will deliver me from this body of Death (*Talaipōros egō anthrōpos! Tis me rhysetai ek tou sōmatos tou thanatou toutou*)? Thanks be to God through Jesus Christ our Lord (Romans 7:24–25)!

## "Who will deliver me from this body of Death?" (v. 24)

The phrase *sōma tou thanatou* ("body of Death") is grammatically ambiguous, but the most plausible sense is a genitive of source—"the body belonging to Death." Greek discourse regularly used such expressions to mark possession or origin by a ruling force rather than mere description. In this idiom, inner faculties or embodied life could be framed as belonging to whatever power exercised control over them, especially when that agency appeared overwhelmed. Such language portrays the person not as morally mistaken but as claimed territory, a self space that is defined by the power that inhabits and directs it. These constructions therefore function to express domination, captivity, and identity under an external rule rather than simple metaphor or poetic flourish within the human subject.

Paul is thus not saying that the body *is* Death, as though physical embodiment were itself the problem. That interpretation—common in later Platonic readings that treat the body (*sōma*) as a prison (*sēma*) for the soul (cf. Plato, *Phaedo* 61e-62c)—misses Paul's realism. For Paul, the body is not a trap to escape. In itself, the human body is good and the site of God's future transformation (Romans 8:11, 23). The problem is not embodiment, but occupation: the body has become the territory Death currently claims as its own (Gaventa, 2011; 2016; 2024; Chesnutt, 1995; Segal, 1994). The body is sacred architecture. So, the problem is not the building itself but the tenant inside the building. "Death," in other words, is not the flesh—it is the force that occupies it.

This distinction sets Paul apart from the Hellenistic moralism found in *Wisdom of Solomon* 9:15, which laments that "the perishable body weighs down the soul" (*phtharton gar sōma barunei psychēn*). For the author of *Wisdom*, matter itself is the burden—the body's material composition is the problem, a drag upon the soul's ascent. For Paul, however, the flesh is not in itself the problem, and it is certainly not cursed because of what it is made of. The crisis lies not in matter but in invasion. What corrupts the human condition is the foreign power that has taken up residence within the boundaries of the embodied self. The body is therefore not a material prison but a battleground—a temple designed for indwelling that has been overrun. The enemy is not body but body under occupation—not physicality itself but the forces that have subjected embodied life to chaotic enslavement.

The verb *rhysetai* ("deliver, rescue") confirms this. *Rhysetai* is a liberation verb, used for decisive divine intervention against hostile powers—not for moral effort or self-improvement. In the Septuagint it regularly appears in combat, exorcistic, or battlefield contexts. Thus, we read: "The Lord will rescue (*rhysetai*) me from all afflictions" (Psalm 34:19 LXX), where the psalmist envisions God tearing him free from encircling threats. Or again, "The Lord stood by me and rescued (*erhysato*) me from the lion's mouth" (2 Timothy 4:17–18), echoing the imagery of Daniel's deliverance as a violent extraction from predatory danger. The term appears in 2 Samuel 12:7 LXX, where God reminds David, "I delivered you from the hand of Saul," framing kingship as rescue from a predatory power that sought his life. Paul's choice of *rhysetai* here is no accident: he is not asking who will *help him behave* better. He is crying out to the one who will pull him out—who will tear him loose from the occupying force that has taken his body hostage.

Paul's question is not philosophical. He's not asking, "How can I become virtuous?" It is liturgical and apocalyptic (Schweitzer, 1931). He is asking, "Who will snatch me from this possessing power?" The cry belongs to the register of Israel's laments: "Out of the depths I cry to you, O Lord" (Psalm 130:1), and likewise, "Rescue me quickly, O Lord, for my spirit fails" (Psalm 143:7 LXX). It is the wail of one overwhelmed, one besieged, one possessed and crying out for deliverance—not the reflection of a moralist who merely wishes he could make better decisions. It is the voice of someone pinned beneath a power greater than himself, summoning the only one strong enough to pull him free.

In this sense, Romans 7 ends where the Psalms of deliverance begin. The "I" of the passage has moved from analysis to invocation. Grammar gives way to groaning. The Law has done its work—it has exposed Sin, unmasked the squatter, revealed the full extent of the captivity. Now there is only one thing left to do: call for rescue.

Paul's phrasing—"Who will deliver me?" (*tis me rhysetai*, Romans 7:24)—is significant. The question assumes that deliverance cannot come from within. The "I" has been exhausted as an agent. Every attempt to obey, every flicker of willing, has failed. The only hope is an external liberator, a stronger presence who can do what the "I" cannot.

98

### "Thanks be to God through Jesus Christ our Lord" (v. 25)

The answer to his own question comes abruptly, almost as a doxological interruption:

> Thanks be to God through Jesus Christ our Lord" (*charis de tō theō dia Iēsou Christou tou kyriou hēmōn*, Romans 7:25).

The abrupt switch from lament to thanksgiving is so sudden that some commentators have wondered if Paul has momentarily stepped out of the monologue to speak as himself again. But that is precisely the point. Deliverance breaks into the monologue from outside. The grammar of captivity gives way to the grammar of praise. In this moment, Paul seems to sit back, having exhausted himself in his cries for deliverance, to realize that he is not helpless after all. There's a new Lord (*kurios*) in town, and while Sin and Death are still surely present, their reign has ended, and their powers are waning.

The phrase "thanks be to God" (*charis de tō theō*) functions here not as polite conclusion but as an exorcistic formula. In ancient Jewish and Greco-Roman ritual texts, invoking the name of a superior power was the means of expelling an inferior one. In the Aramaic incantation bowls from late antiquity, the practitioner drives out a tormenting spirit by declaring lines along the line of "in the name of [X] I adjure you," after which the demon is compelled to depart. The same pattern appears in the Greek Magical Papyri, where the exorcist invokes the divine name above all names to force a hostile entity to flee. Even in the Babylonian *Maqlū* series, the sufferer cries out the divine names of Shamash and Marduk as acts of ritual expulsion (*Maqlū* II). The pattern is consistent: name the affliction, cry for deliverance, invoke the divine Name. Paul's doxology mirrors that liturgical rhythm. By naming "Jesus Christ our Lord," he names the higher authority whose presence drives out the usurper.

The preposition *dia* ("through") is crucial: "through Jesus Christ." Deliverance is not only by God's decree but through the agency and within the presence of the Messiah himself. Paul draws here on the "stronger man" motif that Jesus himself used in Mark 3:27: "No one can enter the house of the strong man and plunder his goods, unless he first binds the strong man." Sin and Death are the "strong man," and Christ is the stronger invader who enters, binds, and liberates the house. The imagery fits perfectly with Paul's possession theology. Deliverance is not escape from the house but repossession of it.

The transition from Romans 7:25 to Romans 8 continues this logic seamlessly. The same verb *oikei*—"to dwell"—that described Sin's indwelling in Romans 7:17 reappears in Romans 8:9–11, but now with a new subject. As Paul declares, "The Spirit of God dwells in you" (*pneuma theou oikei en hymin*, Romans 8:9; cf. *oikei en hymin* again in 8:11). The tenant has changed, and the haunted house has become a temple again. This is why Romans 7, though it ends in a cry of despair, does so only grammatically. Narratively, it opens the door to the invasion of the new inhabitant. The exorcism has begun, but the new inhabitant has yet to be fully described.

Paul's final line is not a regression but a moment of realism. Here, he writes:

> So then, I myself serve the law of God with my mind, but with my flesh I serve the law of Sin (*autos egō tō men noi douleuō nomō theou, tē de sarki nomō hamartias*, Romans 7:25b).

Deliverance has been named but not yet consummated. The new Lord has arrived, and the battle within the self rages on, but the final removal of the evil occupant has yet to happen. The battle of tenants continues until the Spirit moves in fully. The stronger man has been identified, and the house's title deed has changed hands. The "I" still lives in occupied territory, but the victory has been declared.

In short, Romans 7:24–25 is not a lament of failure but a hinge of transformation. It is the final groan of the haunted before the exorcist enters. Paul's theology of salvation turns precisely here—from self-analysis to Spirit invasion—from slavery to repossession. The haunted body becomes holy ground again.

And with the first breath of Romans 8, the haunted house is flooded with light. Thus, Paul can proclaim, with relief: "There is therefore now no condemnation for those who are in Christ Jesus."

## THE SPIRIT AS COUNTER-OCCUPIER (ROMANS 8:1–11)

What follows Paul's tortured cries of Romans 7 is an oft-quoted but misunderstood declaration in Romans 8. As Paul explains:

> There is therefore now no condemnation (*ouden … katakrima*) for those who are in Christ Jesus (*en Christō Iēsou*). For the law of the Spirit of life (*ho gar nomos tou pneumatos tēs zōēs*) in Christ Jesus (*en Christō Iēsou*) has set you free (*eleutherōsen se*) from the law of Sin and Death (*apo tou nomou tēs hamartias kai tou thanatou*, Romans 8:1–2).

With these words, Paul pivots from utter despair to deliverance. The grammar of captivity gives way to the grammar of resurrection. The key terms of Romans 7 return—but they are inverted. The same *nomos* ("law"), the same verbs of indwelling (*oikei*), and the same embodied conflict now reappear under new management.

What Romans 7 described as occupation by Sin and Death, Romans 8 presents as repossession by the Spirit of God.

### The New Law of the Spirit (vv. 1–2)

Paul opens with the famous declarative:

> Therefore, there is now no condemnation (*ouden ara nun katakrima*, Romans 8:1).

The adverb *nun* ("now") marks eschatological time: a decisive shift of epoch, not mood. It's not just that Paul finds relief from his own inability to behave properly. It's more that he rejoices knowing that the new Lord has taken up residence within his body, and that he is no longer on his own in the battle against Sin and Death. The "now" follows the exorcistic cry of 7:24–25. The occupant has been named and judged, and condemnation no longer applies. *Katakrima* denotes not only guilt but the execution of a sentence. The verdict is overturned because the authority in the house has changed.

Verse 2 explains how:

> The Law (*nomos*) of the Spirit of life in Christ Jesus has set you free (*ēleutherōsen*) from the Law of Sin and Death.

Paul uses *nomos* here in parallel to 7:21–23, where two "laws" waged war inside the self. The conflict continues, but the hierarchy has shifted. The "law of the Spirit of life" (*nomos tou pneumatos tēs zōēs*) functions as a counter-law, an anti-Sin, a new ruling order that displaces the previous administration.

The verb *ēleutherōsen* ("has set free") is in the aorist—decisive liberation whose results continue. The same Spirit that raised Jesus (v. 11) has already begun to dismantle the old regime within the believer. The structure of the sentence evokes Exodus language: the Spirit acts as a new Moses leading humanity out from the Pharaohs of Sin and Death.

As we've seen already, the ancient world often depicted chaos forces in duos. In the ancient myths, that is, chaos is always two-handed—disaster comes not from a single agent but from a wicked partnership between Death and disorder. Thus, we've looked at Mōt and Shapshu in Ugaritic myth, where Death (Mōt) devours gods and mortals while the sun-goddess (Shapshu) mediates between realms (KTU 1.6), and Tiamat and Kingu in the Babylonian *Enuma Elish*, where the sea-dragon Tiamat and her lieutenant Kingu unleash cosmic disorder (Tablet I–II). Paul's "Spirit of life" stands as the theological antithesis of the twofold agents of chaos, namely, Sin and Death. The Breath that hovers over the waters of Genesis 1 now re-enters the human microcosm, restoring creation from within, subduing chaos as in the beginning (Genesis 1:2), and bringing order out of disorder once more.

### What the Law Could Not Do (vv. 3–4)

Paul picks up once more with another remark about the dire state he endures as a fleshly creature:

> For what the Law could not do, weakened as it was through the flesh, God did by sending His own Son in the likeness of sinful flesh (*en homoiōmati sarkos hamartias*) and for Sin (*peri hamartias*). He condemned Sin in the flesh (*katekrinen tēn hamartian en tē sarki*), so that the righteous requirement of the Law might be fulfilled in us (*hina to dikaiōma tou nomou plērōthē en hēmin*) who walk not according to the flesh but according to the Spirit (*mē kata sarka peripatousin alla kata pneuma*, Romans 8:3–4).

Paul repeats this same incarnational logic in the so-called "Christ Hymn" of Philippians 2:6–11, where the Son, "though being in the form of God (*en morphē theou*), emptied himself (*ekenōsen*), taking the form of a servant, being made in the likeness of humanity (*en homoiōmati anthrōpōn*)." The deliberate repetition of *homoiōma* in both texts— Romans 8:3 and Philippians 2:7—is not coincidental. It marks continuity of thought: Christ's "likeness" is the same mortal substance (*sarx*) into which Sin had intruded yet now rendered holy by the Spirit's occupancy.

Paul's precision avoids both Docetism—the claim that Jesus only *appeared* human—and the notion of inherited sinfulness in his flesh. His incarnation is not simulation but surgical realism: divine life entering infected matter without contracting the disease. The Son assumes *sarx*—the vulnerable, dying tissue of humanity—but without the parasite of Sin dwelling in it. Paul makes a similar claim to the Corinthians: "He made him who knew no Sin to be Sin for us" (2 Corinthians 5:21). In this way, Paul imagines the incarnation as ontological infiltration, not moral imitation: the divine presence re-entering mortal dust to reclaim it from within.

By saying that God "condemned Sin in the flesh" (*katekrinen tēn hamartian en tē sarki*), Paul declares a judicial reversal that mirrors and completes the exorcism described in Romans 7. The noun *katakrima* ("condemnation") in 8:1 is now turned into its verbal counterpart *katekrinen*: the very act of judging. The location phrase *en tē sarki* is not incidental—it specifies the arena of judgment. Sin is executed in the same realm it once ruled. What the Law could expose but not eliminate, God himself has entered to destroy. The tricky remark in Colossians likewise asserts that the hostile powers have been "disarmed" (*apekdysamenos/apekdysamenoi*, depending on textual alignment) and "publicly shamed" (*edeigmatisen*, Colossians 2:14–15). The "flesh" (*sarx*) thus becomes paradoxical, as it is both the crime scene and the courtroom, the battlefield and the place of victory.

Paul's syntax in verses 3–4 forms a rhetorical chiasm—a poetic and structural device, familiar from both Hebrew parallelism and Greco-Roman rhetoric, in which elements are arranged in an inverted sequence (A–B–B′–A′) to create a mirror structure.

A. The Law's incapacity through the flesh
   B. God sending His Son in likeness of sinful flesh
   B′. God condemning Sin in the flesh
A′. The Law's requirement fulfilled in those walking according to the Spirit.

Such a pattern emphasizes cosmic and anthropological reversal. The movement down into incarnation (B) is matched by the movement up into fulfillment (B′), dramatizing how God undoes within Christ what Sin had done within humanity. The structure itself dramatizes the reality that Sin's weapon (flesh) becomes the site of its own undoing.

Paul continues: "So that the righteous requirement of the Law might be fulfilled in us who walk not according to the flesh but according to the Spirit" (*hina to dikaiōma tou nomou plērōthē en hēmin tois mē kata sarka peripatousin alla kata pneuma*, Romans 8:4). The key phrase *hina to dikaiōma tou nomou plērōthē en hēmin* frames obedience not as abolition but as teleological completion. *Plērōthē* (aorist passive subjunctive of *pleroō*) means "to bring to its full measure," the same verb used in Matthew 5:17 for Jesus' "fulfilling" (*plērōsai*) the Law. Likewise, Paul's claim in Romans 10:4 that "Christ is the telos of the Law" (*telos nomou*) underscores that the Law's intended outcome—its goal, not its cancellation—is internal participation in divine life. The Law is fulfilled not by us but in us, precisely as the Spirit animates human bodies toward righteousness from the inside out.

The participial phrase "who walk not according to flesh (*kata sarka*) but according to Spirit (*kata pneuma*)" translates behavioral language into cosmological orientation. *Kata* denotes not merely manner or behavior but governing accordance or allegiance—it signifies a life lived "under the rule of" either Sin/flesh or Spirit. In other words, Paul frames ethical behavior as metaphysical alignment (cf. Rabens, 2013; 2014a; 2014b; Rehfeld, 2012). To act *kata sarka* is to live from the logic of the old occupant (Sin/flesh), and to do so is to give power, within one's body, to the very forces of Sin and Death. To act *kata pneuma* is, on the contrary, to cooperate with the new tenant's renovation of the house, and thus to give power to the Spirit.

This carries profound implications for understanding "sins." The plural acts, or "sins" (*hamartiai*), are not the same as the singular Power, or "Sin" (*hamartia*). The former are the outworkings of allegiance to the latter. Or think of it like this. Each human action strengthens one indweller or the other. That is, the more a person acts in alignment with the will of Sin and Death, the more that person will be overtaken by Sin and Death. Eventually, this person will come to embody the true essence and desires of these insidious forces. However, the more a person who is filled with the Spirit seeks to behave according to the Spirit's desires, the more that person will continue to be—to share in the existence and desires of—the Spirit. Paul states this elsewhere in Galatians 5:16–25, where "walking by the Spirit" (*pneumati peripateite*, Galatians 5:16) nullifies the "desires of the flesh" (*epithymian sarkos*, Galatians 5:16).

Human behavior is critically important because each person becomes participatory in the cosmic conflict. To "commit sins" is not, in itself, what makes Christ's redemptive work necessary, nor is it reason for doctrines or Gospel messaging that emphasizes shame and guilt. Rather, human behavior is important because, in our actions, we either give more power to Sin and Death in our bodies (by "sinning") or to the Spirit and to Christ (by acting like Jesus). To "sin" is not merely to violate a code and make God angry. It is instead to reinforce the infrastructure of a defeated tyrant. Conversely, each act of love, mercy, sacrifice, or self-control amplifies the Spirit's reign within.

In this sense, Paul's ethic is ontological rather than moralistic (Rabens, 2013; 2014a; 2014b; Rehfeld, 2012). The believer's deeds are extensions of the tenant who occupies their frame. The verb *oikeō* ("to dwell")—used of Sin in Romans 7:17 and of the Spirit in 8:9–11—underscores this indwelling continuity. So, the question is never, "Are you good enough?" It is instead, "Who is living here now?"

Thus, "the righteous requirement of the Law" is fulfilled not by human performance but by participatory alignment. Obedience is no longer an external duty but a symptom of interior transformation—the overflow of divine presence. When Paul speaks of the Law's requirement being "fulfilled in us" (*plērōthē en hēmin*), he envisions human bodies as vessels of realized righteousness, their very actions animated by the indwelling Spirit. This is reminiscent of Ezekiel 36:26–27 LXX, where God declares, "I will put my Spirit within you (*dōsō to pneuma mou en hymin*) and cause you to walk in my statutes" (*poiēsō hina en tois dikaiōmasin mou poreuesthe*).

To sin (lowercase-S), then, is not simply to break a rule. It is to lend energy to the exiled Power still seeking habitation within our bodies, to reopen the door through which Christ has already expelled Sin and Death. To walk in the Spirit is not moral perfection but *synergeia*—co-operation with the divine Spirit inside us and with the renovation already in motion. This recalls Paul's encouragement to the Philippians to "work out your salvation" (*tēn heautōn sōtērian katergazesthe*) ... "for it is God who works in you" (*theos gar estin ho energōn en hymin*, Philippians 2:12–13). With the Spirit inside, human life becomes sacramental. It is the visible manifestation of whichever Presence holds the house. And in those who have united with Christ's body, the rightful Owner has already reclaimed the keys.

### Flesh-Mind vs. Spirit-Mind (vv. 5–8)

Paul's next contrast is between the "flesh-mind" (*phronēma tēs sarkos*, Romans 8:6a) and the "spirit-mind" (*phronēma tou pneumatos*, v. 6b).

> For those who are according to the flesh (*kata sarka*) set their minds on the things of the flesh (*ta tēs sarkos*), but those who are according to the Spirit (*kata pneuma*) set their minds on the things of the Spirit (*ta tou pneumatos*). For the mind of the flesh (*to de phronēma tēs sarkos*) is Death, but the mind of the Spirit (*to phronēma tou pneumatos*) is life and peace. Because the mind of the flesh (*to phronēma tēs sarkos*) is hostile to God. It does not submit to God's Law (*nomō tou theou*), indeed it cannot. Those who are in the flesh (*en sarki ontes*) cannot please God (*theō aresai*, Romans 8:5–8).

This contrast extends the language of possession into cognition. The noun *phronēma* ("mindset, orientation") denotes not thoughts but the governing disposition—the controlling atmosphere of the self, what ancient Stoics sometimes described as the *hēgemonikon* ("ruling faculty") and what Paul recasts as the internal sovereignty of either Spirit or Sin. In Paul's usage, *phronēma* names a condition shaped by the power one lives under, not an interior mental state freely generated by the self, reinforcing his point that this is not psychology but dominion. Regarding these opposing orientations, Paul asserts plainly,

"The mind of the flesh is Death (*thanatos*), but the mind of the Spirit is life and peace" (*zōē kai eirēnē*, Romans 8:6).

The opposition here is not dualistic in the Greek philosophical sense. *Sarx* ("flesh") does not mean material body but the human organism under foreign control—Sin's occupation regime. *Pneuma*, by contrast, is not mere "spirit" or "soul" in some later theological sense. Paul's categories are simply not that neat and tidy. *Pneuma* is divine life-breath indwelling that human organism. Paul's anthropology is thus not body vs. soul but tenant vs. tenant. It's about the opposing entities inhabiting the human self—Sin and Death vs. divine Spirit. And the *phronēma* ("mind") simply follows whoever holds the lease.

Verse 7 personifies the fleshly mind: "It does not submit to the Law of God, nor indeed is it capable of doing so" (*ouch hypotassetai oude gar dynatai*). The impossibility is ontological, not motivational. Under the wrong indweller, obedience is not just unlikely—it is structurally impossible. The self cannot offer what it does not possess. This coheres with the Qumran dualism of the *Community Rule* (1QS 3–4), where each human life is governed either by the spirit of truth (*rūaḥ 'emet*) or the spirit of perversity (*rūaḥ ha-ʿavlā*), and conduct follows inevitably from whichever spirit holds sway. There is no autonomous middle ground, no neutral psychological terrain. Paul stands within this same ancient logic, namely, that behavior follows habitation, and sovereignty determines action.

For Paul, then, life according to the Spirit (*kata pneuma*) is not about moral improvement but about a new indwelling configuration. The "mind of the Spirit" is consciousness re-wired by occupancy. Where the Law once functioned externally as command, the Spirit now functions internally as impulse. God's promise to "put my Law within them" (Jeremiah 31:33) is realized not through moral recall but through indwelling presence.

### The Spirit Dwelling Within (vv. 9–11)

The next verses make explicit what has been implicit all along:

> But you are not in the flesh (*ouk este en sarki*) but in the Spirit (*alla en pneumati*), if indeed the Spirit of God dwells in you (*pneuma theou oikei en hymin*). Anyone who does not have the Spirit of Christ (pneuma Christou) does not belong to him (*houtos ouk estin autou*). But if Christ is in you (*ei de Christos en hymin*), though the body is dead because of Sin (*to men sōma nekron dia hamartian*), the Spirit is life because of righteousness (*to de pneuma zōē dia dikaiosynēn*). And if the Spirit of him who raised Jesus from the dead dwells in you

(*ei de to pneuma tou egeirantos ton Iēsoun ek nekrōn oikei en hymin*), he who raised Christ from the dead (*ho egeiras Christon ek nekrōn*) will also give life (*zōopoiēsei*) to your mortal bodies (*ta thnēta ta sōmata hymōn*) through his Spirit dwelling in you (*dia tou enoikountos autou pneumatos en hymin*, Romans 8:9–11).

The repetition of *oikei* ("dwells") three times in vv. 9–11 is the lexical hinge between Romans 7 and 8. Sin "dwells" in Paul (7:17), while the Spirit "dwells" in believers (8:9–11). The same verb, the same house, but a new tenant. Paul's theology of salvation is literally a change of occupancy (Gaventa, 2011; 2016; 2024).

The conditional *ei per* ("if indeed") introduces not so much as a doubt, but more of a recognition. It is the ancient rhetorical way of saying, "and you know this to be the case," or "you know I'm right about this." The test of possession is presence. To be "in the Spirit" (*en pneumati*, Romans 8:9) is to have the Spirit "in you" (*oikei en hymin*, Romans 8:9–11). Paul frames both sides of the relationship with spatial prepositions because for him union with God is a matter of shared dwelling space, not abstract metaphysics.

This mutual indwelling parallels the Johannine *en emoi/en hymin* formulas—Jesus' own language of reciprocal habitation: "Abide in me, and I in you" (John 15:4–5). Early Christian vocabulary for salvation consistently assumes a spatial anthropology. Human beings are not defined primarily by virtues, vices, or even moral history, but by occupancy. A person is what—or who—dwells inside one's self space.

As we've seen, for Paul, the self is a space, a locus of habitation. Like his fellow Second Temple Jewish thinkers, he viewed the human as sacred architecture—dust and breath united to form a temple whose meaning derives from the presence within it. Paul stands squarely in that tradition. His language of *oikeō* ("to dwell"), *enoikeō* ("to indwell"), and *katoikeō* ("to settle, inhabit") is not metaphor but ontology. It expresses how he conceives the human self as a kind of porous, inhabitable realm (cf. Putthoff, 2017).

In his letters, the "inner human" (*ho esō anthrōpos*) is not a psychological interior but a spatial one—the chamber where rival powers seek residence (Romans 7:22; 2 Corinthians 4:16). To be "in the flesh" (*en sarki*) is to inhabit a realm whose boundaries have been breached by Sin and Death. To be "in the Spirit" (*en pneumati*) is to inhabit a new realm because the new realm now inhabits you. The direction goes both ways because the reality goes both ways.

This means Paul's soteriology is inseparable from his spatial anthropology: salvation is re-habitation. It is not the elevation of virtue or the improvement of moral capacity. It is the Spirit taking up residence where another power once lived. The "I" does not merely believe differently. The "I" becomes different because the occupied space has changed occupants.

Thus, when Paul says, "If indeed the Spirit of God dwells in you," he is not asking for introspection. He is naming the single condition that defines Christian existence, namely, who lives in the house of the self? The Gospel's answer is that the stronger one lives here now.

Romans 8:10 clarifies the paradox: "If Christ is in you, though the body is dead because of Sin, the Spirit is life because of righteousness" (Romans 8:10). The phrase *to sōma nekron* ("the body [is] dead") does not mean the body is worthless or evil. It names the body's current mortal condition—still marked by the lingering residue of Death's regime (*thanatos*). Paul's realism is striking. Even with "Christ in you" (*Christos en hymin*), the body remains a space shaped by its past occupancy. Mortality still clings to it. The flesh still bears the scars of former tenancy. The old regime has been dethroned, but its aftereffects remain, like structural damage in a house long inhabited by violent squatters.

And yet, even within that decaying architecture, a new life-force pulses. "The Spirit is life" (*to pneuma zōē*) is a radical ontological claim, a declaration that the Spirit functions as embodied vitality, resurrection in seed form. The indwelling Spirit is not merely an influence but a down payment (*arrabōn*, cf. 2 Corinthians 1:22; 5:5), an installed future, the life of the age to come already embedded inside perishable matter. Paul therefore pictures believers as living paradoxes, perishable bodies hosting imperishable Presence, mortal flesh housing immortal Breath.

This is why he contrasts "the body being dead because of Sin" with "the Spirit being life because of righteousness" (*dikaiosynē*). *Dikaiosynē* here means not ethical behavior but right alignment—the rectifying work God has accomplished in Christ. The Spirit's presence is the evidence that righteousness has already begun its work of re-creation. The believer's body remains subject to decay, yet the indwelling Spirit is already transforming that same body from the inside out. Resurrection has begun—not yet in full, but as an active power, a new occupant reshaping the very space still marked by Death.

In Paul's imagination, this means Christians live in an interim condition. We have one foot in Adam's world and one foot in Christ's. The body still groans, but the Spirit groans with it (Romans 8:23, 26). The house still creaks with traces of its former tenant, but the new inhabitant has already begun renovations. Christ in you means that the future has moved into the present. The Spirit is the life of the resurrection inhabiting a body still haunted by flashbacks of Death.

The climactic promise of Romans 8:11 completes the reversal of the horror of Romans 7:

> He who raised Jesus from the dead will give life to your mortal bodies through his Spirit dwelling in you (*dia tou enoikountos autou pneumatos en hymin*, Romans 8:11).

The invader who once metastasized Death is replaced by the indweller who animates Life. The same *pneuma* ("Spirit") that raised Jesus from the tomb now occupies human flesh as resurrection energy in progress. In mythic terms, Māwet has been swallowed—Death itself is digested by the divine Breath.

Paul's realism remains embodied: the "mortal bodies" (*thnēta sōmata*) do not vanish but are transfigured from within. Salvation is not escape from the body but its re-animation—an internal recreation echoing Genesis 2:7, where God breathed into the dust-figure, and it became a living being. Romans 8 is that verse rewritten: God breathes again into the dust-figure, and the indwelling Spirit turns mortal flesh into the earliest stirring of resurrection existence, even in the present life.

## SYNTHESIZED THEOLOGICAL READING

Having walked through the text of Romans 5–8, we can now make some summarizing assertions about our findings.

### Point 1—Sin and Death as Personal Powers

When Paul speaks of Sin and Death, he is not speaking in metaphor. They are animate powers—divine-level agents whose activity recalls the chaos beings of the ancient Near East. In Ugaritic myth, Mōt devours Baal and reigns until the storm-god rises again. In Mesopotamian lore, Tiamat births monsters that turn creation back toward disorder. Paul's "Sin" and "Death" behave with the same vitality and appetite. They seize, deceive, rule, kill (Romans 5–7). They are not metaphors for wrongdoing or mortality. They function as cosmic rulers, active powers that dominate bodies, redirect agency, and impose bondage upon human flesh through violent occupation from within.

Jewish tradition had already begun to name these forces: *Wisdom of Solomon* 2:24 blames "the envy of the devil" for Death's entrance. *1 Enoch* 15–16 imagines demonic spirits born from the Nephilim, roaming and indwelling human bodies. Paul's cosmos belongs to this same symbolic world but compresses it inward. Instead of devouring the world from the outside, the monsters have moved inside human flesh. Sin becomes the invasive serpent coiled within the body. Death sits enthroned in the members, ruling like Māwet in the underworld of the self.

For Paul, the Law (*nomos*) provided the doorway that these powers exploited. It was holy, yet like the divine speech of creation in Mesopotamian myth, it could be twisted into a new instrument of chaos. The command that promised life "became Death to me," Paul laments (Romans 7:10). The monsters hijacked the good. In this, Paul stands neither as a rational moralist nor a modern evangelist, but as an ancient myth-maker, diagnosing humanity's plight in terms of rival gods occupying divine territory—in this case, that territory just happens to be the bounded space of the human self.

### Point 2—The Human as Hybrid Vessel

At the core of this worldview lies Genesis 2:7. After bringing order out of disorder, cosmos out of chaos, "the Lord God formed the human from the dust of the ground and breathed into his nostrils the breath of life." Humanity is a deliberate fusion of opposites—earth and breath, matter and spirit, mortal and divine (Putthoff, 2020). Ancient readers would have recognized in this not an abstract creation story but a statement about ontology—about what it means to be human. To be human is to be porous. The self is not sealed, but it is a type of space whose boundaries are permeable and whose form and shape are malleable. It is not rigid, and its shape comes to mimic that of whomever resides within it—in this case, it either mimics Sin and Death or the Spirit of Christ.

This anthropology pervades Scripture. When God's Spirit fills a person—Bezalel crafting the tabernacle (Exodus 31:3, *'ămallē' 'ōtō rūaḥ 'ĕlōhīm*) or the prophets speaking the divine word (Micah 3:8; cf. Ezekiel 2:2)—the result is glory. When that breath withdraws, chaos rushes in. Ezekiel 10 pictures the Glory departing the Temple, and immediately the city becomes prey to fire and sword. The same pattern governs the individual body. When the rightful Indweller is not present, vacancy itself becomes invitation. Within the logic presupposed by *Maqlū*, the absence of protective divine presence leaves persons and spaces exposed to invasive forces such. Monstrosity is the spiritual equivalent of rot: where life withdraws, decomposition fills the gap.

Paul therefore describes the human not as neutral moral agent but as contested architecture. The verb *oikeō*—"to dwell"—is his key. In

Romans 7, Sin "dwells in me" (*oikousa en emoi hamartia*, Romans 7:17). In Romans 8, the Spirit "dwells in you" (*pneuma theou oikei en hymin*, Romans 8:9–11). The difference between the sinner and the saint is not effort, not attempting to be better or "sin" less. The difference is occupancy. Humanity is hybrid by design and haunted by possibility: the same clay that can house the divine Breath can also host the breath of Death.

This explains Paul's realism about flesh. *Sarx* ("flesh") is not *evil* material but *vulnerable* material—the human frame itself is morally neutral, but the problem is that it is capable of possession. As such, its behavior is also highly impressionable and easily swayed by the power inhabiting it. The human body is therefore not discarded in salvation, because it is not ultimately the problem. It's repossessed, and its circuits are rewired by new energy. The result is what we might call *haunted holiness*: the temple is cleansed but still trembling, the vessel is fragile yet filled again with fire.

### Point 3—Christ and Spirit as Counter-Occupiers

The climax of Paul's argument arrives when the stronger tenant moves in. Romans 8 is not a change of metaphor but a change of management. The same architectural vocabulary persists: the Law of Sin and Death once dwelt in the members, but now the Spirit of life dwells within, giving life to mortal bodies.

Christ himself is the prototype of this indwelling reversal, hence: "God sent his own Son in the likeness of sinful flesh" (Romans 8:3). The divine Son entered the infected realm without becoming infected. In him, the old powers met their end. Sin was "condemned in the flesh," executed on its own turf. The cross is therefore not merely substitution but eviction, as the usurper (Sin) has been cast out of the very medium (flesh) it dominated.

The Spirit continues that victory as ongoing occupation. In Jewish apocalyptic texts, deliverance often meant expulsion of demons, while for Paul, it means the replacement of the invading forces by the Spirit of God himself. There is no neutral self between exorcism and infilling: "If anyone does not have the Spirit of Christ, he does not belong to him" (Romans 8:9). Salvation is not the escape from embodiment. It is its repurposing, as the haunted house has become the Holy of Holies once more. The human self is once more the site of the glorious dwelling of God's presence, just as God had always intended it to be.

This is why Paul's Gospel cannot be reduced to justification by faith in a forensic sense alone. The entirety of his narrative points to ontological warfare. The Gospel cannot be reduced to paperwork, either. That is, it is not merely an angry God begrudgingly dismissing the case against a guilty offender who now has a high-powered lawyer at his side. It's about power. We cannot reduce the Spirit to a metaphor for moral insight, because Paul makes it clear: the Spirit is a living agent performing re-animation within the believer's mortal, fallen, decaying frame. Resurrection begins inside. The breath that raised Jesus already circulates through human lungs, driving out the residual fumes of Death.

In cosmic terms, this is the final inversion of the ancient *Chaoskampf*. The war between Creator and monsters is now fought within the bounds of the human self. Christ's indwelling Spirit is the storm-god within the clay, the divine wind that re-creates order where the sea of chaos once raged. This is why Paul can declare that anyone who is in Christ is the site of new creation (*kainē ktisis*, 2 Corinthians 5:17).

## *FROM OCCUPATION TO INDWELLING*

Romans 5–8 brings Paul's theology of the human condition to its sharpest focus. The self, in his account, is neither an autonomous moral agent nor a static essence, but it is a site of ongoing occupation. Sin and Death are more than metaphors for moral failure. In Paul's view, they are living forces—cosmic squatters whose reign extends all the way down into the members, from the mind, to the body, to the fingertips. Yet the same realism that makes Romans 7 so harrowing makes Romans 8 so hopeful. The haunted house becomes holy ground.

What begins as a lament—"Sin dwelling in me" (7:17)—ends as a confession of new tenancy: "the Spirit of God dwells in you" (8:9). The repetition of "dwelling" language ties the entire argument together. Salvation, for Paul, is less about behavioral correction and more about ontological reversal. The wrong occupant is expelled, and the rightful one moves back in. The self is re-spirited. Where the Law could only expose the intruder, the Spirit reclaims the premises, and the very body that once served as the throne of Death now becomes the dwelling of resurrection life.

This anthropology is as ancient as it is radical. It echoes the world of Genesis 2:7, in which dust becomes a living statue by divine breath, and it reverberates with the old chaos myths of the Near East, where order triumphs only when a stronger deity subdues the monsters of the deep. Paul has not abandoned that mythic imagination. Far from it, he has internalized it. The chaos battle, or *Chaoskampf*, now takes place within human flesh, and the victory unfolds through indwelling.

The pastoral implication follows naturally. If Sin and Death are invasive tenants rather than moral slip-ups, then redemption is not self-improvement but divine repossession. Every act of grace is a new occupation by the Spirit, and every prayer for deliverance is an invitation for the stronger one to stay. The Christian life is not the denial of monstrosity but its transformation—the haunted house filled again with light.

The argument of Romans 5–8 brings us to the threshold of the deepest mystery in Paul's Gospel. If Sin and Death are the monsters that inhabit humanity, then the question that remains is: Who dares to enter their domain and cast them out? As we've seen in this chapter, Paul's vision ends not just with the Spirit repossessing creation but with the startling revelation of the One who makes that repossession possible— the embodied, boundary-breaking Christ. In him, the cosmic drama turns personal and visible. The same struggle that raged within flesh now takes flesh. The war between Life and Death becomes incarnate. What Paul sketches in abstract terms—Sin's eviction and the Spirit's arrival—takes its living form in the crucified and risen Jesus.

So, our story moves forward to a closer look at Jesus himself, at the one who dares to engage in battle with Sin and Death, at the one who has brought liberation to humankind. We turn now from the haunted self to the holy Invader, from the description of possession to the revelation of the Possessor. The next chapter turns to this figure who unites the human and the divine, the dead and the living, the earthly and the heavenly—our monstrous Lord and Savior Jesus Christ, whose very being brings the victory.

# CHAPTER 6—OUR MONSTROUS LORD AND SAVIOR JESUS CHRIST

## CHRIST AS THE DIVINE MONSTER

Jesus the Christ is a monster.

That sentence, without question, sounds offensive, blasphemous, and heretical to modern ears. Yet that reaction itself exposes how deeply we have domesticated both "monster" and "Christ." We hear monster and think of grotesques from cinema. We hear Christ and think of serenity, moral perfection, predictability. But in the ancient world, "monster" did not primarily mean evil. It meant other—that which ruptures categories, disturbs the boundaries of creation, and reminds mortals that the cosmos is not safely contained (Cohen, 1996). A monster was a being of excess and fusion: part this, part that, never wholly either. And by that definition, no figure in Scripture fits the term more completely—or more redemptively—than Jesus of Nazareth, the Christ himself.

In the previous chapter, Paul showed us the human as a haunted vessel: Sin and Death functioning as invasive tenants within the body. In Romans 8, the Spirit entered as the counter-occupier, reclaiming the self as holy ground. But that naturally provokes a question: Who is this Spirit? Whose breath has such authority to drive out gods, to repossess the human temple, to reverse Death's tenancy? Paul's answer is not abstract. The Spirit is the breath of the risen Christ—the One who has already descended into Death's domain, fought the monsters on their own turf, and returned unkillable. The Spirit's power to indwell is borrowed from the Son's power to cross every border and survive it.

To call Christ "monstrous," then, is to recognize the scandal of his crossings. He violates the most inviolable boundaries: between Creator and creature, divinity and dust, life and death, heaven and Sheol (Cohen,

1996). He is the hybrid par excellence—fully divine, fully human, united "without confusion, without division," as Chalcedon would later put it, yet impossible to categorize within the logic of either. Every boundary that monsters threaten to corrupt, Christ crosses to heal. Every liminal space that once belonged to the forces of chaos—womb, wilderness, and tomb—becomes, in him, a site of new creation. The very qualities that make a being monstrous in myth—the ability to transgress and refuse annihilation—become in Christ the instruments of divine mercy.

Gregory of Nyssa writes:

> The Deity was hidden under the veil of our nature, that so, as with ravenous fish, the hook of the Deity might be gulped down along with the bait of flesh, and thus, life being introduced into the house of Death, and light shining in darkness, that which is diametrically opposed to light and life might vanish (*Great Catechism* 24).

Death swallowed what looked like mortal flesh and was torn apart from within.

That is not polite theology—it is visceral, even horrifying imagery. And yet it is exactly the kind of holy horror the Gospel demands: God's victory accomplished through deception of the deceiver, invasion of the invader, monstrosity against monstrosity. The Son of God defeats the devouring powers not by avoiding them but by letting himself be devoured and detonating divinity inside their bowels.

This is why the early Christians spoke of the cross and resurrection in the language of combat and possession. Paul calls Christ's triumph a theatral spectacle in which "the rulers and authorities are disarmed and exposed to public shame" (Colossians 2:15). The author of Hebrews describes him breaking "the power of the one who has the power of Death" (2:14). John sees him as both Lamb and Lion—gentle victim and terrifying victor. Each of these images bears the same paradox: Christ is the being who overturns the cosmic order by embodying it to its limit. He is the holy monster, the divine hybrid who enters the domain of the grotesque to redeem it from the inside out.

So when we name Jesus "Lord," we are confessing more than moral lordship. We are acknowledging a power so boundary-shattering that language strains to contain it. The incarnation is divine trespass. The resurrection is divine refusal to stay buried. The ascension is divine expansion, the body of a crucified man becoming the dwelling space of heaven itself. Every line that separated heaven and earth, human and divine, mortal and immortal, now runs through Jesus—and through those who belong to him.

To say "Jesus the Christ is a monster" is therefore not to profane him—it truly is to praise him. It is to recognize that the God who saves does so by crossing the lines we thought were absolute, by becoming the very hybrid we feared, by transforming the terror of the monstrous into the glory of mercy. He is the divine invader who reclaims the haunted cosmos.

## THE TRAITS OF THE MONSTROUS CHRIST

If monsters are defined by their ability to blur the lines that define reality—by their refusal to stay within the boundaries that keep the world safe—then Christ is the consummate monster. Each of the five traits that, according to my framework, ancient myth and modern theory associate with monstrosity—hybridity, strange origin, terror, liminality, and persistence—appears in him, yet transfigured. What is terrifying in myth becomes salvific in Jesus. What the ancients feared as corruption, Scripture announces as incarnation. Christ embodies every monstrous trait and turns it holy.

### *Monstrous Trait 1—Hybridity: The Incarnate Fusion*

At the heart of monstrosity lies hybridity—the fusing of what should not be joined. In myth, this fusion signals disorder: lion-bodies with human heads, serpents with wings, gods interbreeding with mortals. But in Christ, hybridity becomes the very form of redemption. Paul captures it with surgical precision in Romans 8:3: God sent his Son *en homoiōmati sarkos hamartias*, "in the likeness of sinful flesh." The phrase is easily misunderstood. Paul does not say Christ took on sinful flesh. He says he came *in its likeness*. This is not docetic make-believe, as though Jesus only *appeared* human. It is genuine *sarx*—flesh subject to hunger, fatigue, and death—yet without the indwelling parasite of Sin that Paul described in Romans 7. Christ wears our *sarx* as it was meant to be: matter animated by divine Breath without corruption.

In him, Genesis 2:7 is replayed—the dust and the Breath reunited, the fracture of Adam healed. Where Adam's clay became habitation for the monstrous powers, Christ's body becomes their eviction notice. The ancient theologians of Chalcedon would later capture this mystery in four negations: "without confusion, without change, without division, without separation." It is the classical statement of divine hybridity, a union that defies every rational category. To pagans it sounded absurd. To Christians, it was and is the grammar of salvation.

Mythic literature offers its pale prefigurations. Gilgamesh, two-thirds divine and one-third human, embodied the ancient longing for a boundary-crossed hero who could unite heaven and earth. Christ fulfills that archetype without the corruption. The hybrid who once provoked fear becomes the hybrid who heals. Even the virgin conception—Mary overshadowed by the Spirit (Luke 1:35)—mirrors the ancient stories of gods mingling with mortals but sanctifies the pattern. In this new myth made real, no lust, violence, or chaos births the hybrid—only consent, holiness, and creative speech. Christ is the hybrid done right: not a monster of confusion, but the divine fusion that restores creation's integrity. Only a being who is fully dust and fully Breath can re-knit the torn fabric of dust and Breath that is humanity.

### Monstrous Trait 2—Supernatural Ancestry: The Divine Genealogy

Monsters always have strange births. They emerge from unions that shouldn't happen, born of gods and beasts, mortals and immortals, life and death. The birth of Christ is no less strange, though infinitely holier. John opens his Gospel not with a cradle but with eternity: "In the beginning was the Word, and the Word was with God, and the Word was God… and the Word became flesh" (John 1:1, 14). Luke, by contrast, ends his genealogy with "Adam, son of God" (Luke 3:38). Between the two, we glimpse the impossible lineage: the eternal Word who speaks worlds into being now enters that world through the lineage of Adam. Paul condenses the paradox to a single phrase: "born of a woman" (*genomenon ek gynaikos*, Galatians 4:4). The verb *ginomai*—"to become, to come into being"—marks incarnation as ontological event, not metaphor. God does not just *visit* humanity. He *becomes* humanity.

Ancient readers would have recognized the type. The Akkadian *Legend of Sargon* told of a baby set adrift in a basket and destined for kingship. The Egyptians celebrated Horus, born from Isis after Osiris's death, a divine child conceived amid loss. Every culture, it seems, dreamed of miraculous birth as the signal of a world-changing life. Yet the Gospels invert the pattern. The miraculous conception of Jesus is not the product of divine violence or erotic chaos. It is the product of divine word and human assent. "Let it be to me according to your word," says Mary (Luke 1:38). The monstrosity of Jesus' origin lies in its purity: a birth without precedent, without male seed, without Sin. The hybrid child who once symbolized cosmic disruption now inaugurates cosmic healing.

### Monstrous Trait 3—Terror and Disorder: The Monster Slayer

Wherever Christ acts, fear follows. Mark's Gospel uses the phrase *ephobēthēsan phobon megan*—"they feared a great fear" (Mark 4:41; cf.

5:15; 6:50). The redundant Greek construction magnifies dread: not simply that they feared, but that they were overwhelmed by fear. When Jesus stills the storm, the disciples' terror exceeds what the storm itself provoked. "What type of being is this," they ask, "that even the wind and the sea obey him?" (*potapos estin houtos, hoti kai hoi anemoi kai hē thalassa autō hypakouousin?*, Matthew 8:27; cf. Mark 4:41). The disciples literally ask *what* Jesus is. By defeating the sea before their eyes, he has placed himself in an ancient category of beings that they simply cannot wrap their minds around. The one who commands chaos itself must be more than human—and thus frightening. It's only after his second battle against the sea when the disciples put the pieces together, declaring, "Surely this is Son of God" (*alēthōs theou huios ei*, Matthew 14:33) and placing him in (and above) the ancient category of "sons of gods"—the archetypal monster-slaying heroes of the ancient world.

Everywhere he goes, Christ disrupts the systems that keep the world comfortable. In the Temple he overturns tables and drives out merchants (Mark 11:15–18), a scene that certainly evokes the logic of YHWH's storm-theophanies (cf. Psalm 18): the earth quakes, the heavens thunder, divine anger blazes. The cleansing of the Temple is not a tantrum but the arrival of the monster-slaying storm-god in the flesh, reclaiming his house from corruption. No wonder the authorities plot his death. To them, this boundary-crossing prophet is not reformer but monster—a living breach in the sacred order.

Even the Romans sensed the terror in the illogicality of a crucified deity. Ancient critics mocked Christians for worshipping a god who had been killed (cf. Celsus, *True Doctrine*, in Origen, *Contra Celsum*), an executed criminal raised from the dead. But that, precisely, is the scandalous point. The same logic appears visually in the *Alexamenos Graffito*, a Roman wall carving of a crucified figure with a donkey's head that mocks a Christian named Alexamenos for worshiping "his god." The Christ who terrifies the cosmos does so, in other words, by dying and rising within it. The power that once belonged to the monsters—power to unsettle, to disorient, to upend—is now the mark of divine presence. In Christ, holy terror replaces unholy fear.

### Monstrous Trait 4—Liminality: The Threshold Lord

Monsters haunt the edges of worlds—caves, tombs, seas, deserts—places where categories collapse. Jesus lives his entire story at those edges. He is born among animals outside the human living quarters (Luke 2:7) and dies among criminals outside the city gates (Hebrews

13:12). He preaches from shorelines and mountaintops, prays in wildernesses, and crosses lakes that embodied chaos. Each geography is a theological statement: wherever boundaries divide heaven and earth, purity and impurity, life and death, Jesus stands on the seam.

The Gospels dramatize this visually through the language of tearing. When Jesus is baptized, "the heavens were torn open" (*schizomenous*, Mark 1:10). When he dies, "the veil of the Temple was torn in two" (*eschisthē*, Matthew 27:51). The same verb, *schizō*, binds these moments together. What began as a rip in the sky ends as a rip in the sanctuary veil. Heaven's breach becomes the Temple's breach. In both cases, Christ is the rupture—the living fissure between realms.

Ancient gate myths help frame the image. In the Ugaritic *Baal Cycle*, the god of life must pass through the "Gates of Mōt" to reclaim the living world. In Mesopotamia's *Descent of Ishtar*, the goddess passes seven gates to reach the underworld. Christ seems to fulfill the archetype not by negotiating with Death but by annihilating the gates themselves. "Lift up your heads, O gates," sings the Psalmist (Psalm 24:7 LXX), "and the King of Glory shall come in." The early Church seems to have viewed that as the triumphant entrance of the risen Christ into the underworld's fortress. The threshold is no longer a barrier. It has become his domain. Christ is not only at the threshold—he *is* the threshold.

### Monstrous Trait 5—Persistence: The One Who Will Not Stay Dead

The final mark of the monstrous is persistence—the refusal to remain dead. In horror tales, the monster always returns: the vampire rises at dusk, the zombie horde reawakens, the slasher survives the credits. Paul knows that pattern. He uses *anezēsen*—"came back to life"—to describe Sin in Romans 7:9: "When the commandment came, Sin revived, and I died." Sin, like every mythic monster, is undead, always reanimating when provoked. But in the Gospel, that logic is broken by a different resurrection. The verb changes: Christ *ēgerthē*, "was raised." One reanimation leads to death. The other swallows Death. The undead cycle gives way to unending life.

Patristic writers seized on this inversion. Athanasius wrote that Christ "made Death disappear as straw from fire" (*Inc.* 2.8). Gregory Nazianzen insists that he is buried as man and rises as God (*Oration* 45.24). Christ takes the monster's trick—the repeated return from death—and makes it permanent. The nightmare of endless dying becomes the miracle of endless life, as Christ's resurrection redefines monstrous persistence itself. Death cannot contain him because he is now the indwelling life that fills all things (Ephesians 1:23). The power that once animated the monsters—the restless refusal to die—has been sanctified into immortality. The unkillable now belongs to the holy.

## THE THREE LAYERS OF MONSTROSITY IN CHRIST

Every culture's monsters work on more than one level. They are never just creatures that crawl out of swamps. They are symbols, mirrors, and warnings. In Christ, each layer of monstrosity—cosmic, human, and indwelling—is not only echoed but fulfilled and reversed. What the ancients feared in their monsters, Paul and the early Christians celebrate in their Messiah. He is the monster who does not destroy creation but re-creates it.

### Layer 1—Mythic Function: Christ and the Chaos Powers

At the cosmic level, monstrosity embodies the eternal battle between order and chaos, life and death, creation and uncreation. In the myths of the ancient Near East, this drama unfolds across heaven and sea: Marduk versus Tiamat, Baal versus Mōt, YHWH versus Leviathan. Creation, in those stories, is always born from struggle. The monster must be slain so that life can emerge and continue.

Paul's Christology recasts this mythic combat in apocalyptic realism. The chaos dragon has not disappeared. It has changed its form. Death is now the devourer, Sin its parasitic twin. But the battle no longer plays out across primordial waters—it happens within the body of Christ himself. "Death has been swallowed up in victory," Paul declares (1 Corinthians 15:54), using the LXX verb *katapothē* from Isaiah 25:8: "He will swallow up Death forever." The old *Chaoskampf* verbs—swallow, crush, destroy—are now verbs of resurrection.

In Colossians 1:15–20, the mythic dimension reaches its climax. Christ is the "firstborn of all creation," the one "through whom all things were made… things visible and invisible, whether thrones or dominions or rulers or authorities." These cosmic hierarchies are not abstractions. They are Paul's version of the old pantheon, the divine and semi-divine beings who populate the heavens. And yet, he says, "He disarmed the rulers and authorities and made a public spectacle of them" (Colossians 2:15). The chaos gods have been paraded as prisoners. The monster that once threatened old creation has become its raw material for new creation.

For Paul, the resurrection is the final mythic act—the monster slain from the inside out, the corpse of Death turned into the seed of life. What the *Enuma Elish* imagined symbolically, Christ accomplishes historically (Putthoff, 2020). Creation is not carved from the monster's body. Creation itself is resurrected from the body of the monster-slayer.

## Layer 2—Anthropological Function: Christ and the Fractured Human

At the anthropological level, monsters have always been mirrors. They show us the cracks in our own reflection, the parts of ourselves we disown. The vampire, the werewolf, the possessed child—these are not strangers; they are us, dramatized. That is precisely Paul's point in Romans 7–8. Humanity is a haunted species, divine breath entangled in dust, bearing God's likeness and presence yet hosting his rivals.

Christ enters this fractured condition "in the likeness of sinful flesh" (Romans 8:3). The Greek phrase *en homoiōmati sarkos hamartias* is theological dynamite. Here, Paul means that Christ becomes what we are without becoming what inhabits us. He takes the physical form of our invaded humanity but without being invaded by the invader. The possessed condition of Romans 7—"it is no longer I, but Sin dwelling in me" (v. 17)—is reversed in Christ. He alone is the un-possessed human and the uncorrupted host.

In doing so, Christ does not simply sympathize, but he actually repairs. His body is the prototype of healed embodiment, the one in whom divine and human coexist without rivalry. The hybrid monstrosity that once terrified—dust animated by divine power—now becomes the instrument of salvation. Paul's anthropology, seen through Christ, is not that of guilt and pardon but of infection and cure. The self that was once the monster's house becomes again the dwelling of God.

## Layer 3—Cosmological Function: Christ as the Indwelling Power

Finally, at the deepest and most intimate level, monstrosity involves possession. The monster does not merely attack from without. It inhabits, speaks through, animates. In Paul's theology, this layer is not erased but redeemed. Christ becomes the new indweller—the holy possessor. "It is no longer I who live, but Christ who lives in me" (Galatians 2:20). "Christ is in you," Paul tells the Romans, "and the Spirit of God dwells in you" (Romans 8:9–10). To the Colossians, he calls this reality "the mystery hidden for ages... which is Christ in you, the hope of glory" (Colossians 1:27).

These paired expressions—*en Christō* ("in Christ") and *Christos en hymin* ("Christ in you")—form a symmetrical theology of habitation. The prepositions flip back and forth like mirrors facing each other. The believer is in Christ even as Christ is in the believer. Salvation, therefore, is not a transaction but a relocation—mutual indwelling between God and human. The Greek pattern continues in the Johannine writings: "Abide in me, and I in you" (*meinate en emoi kagō en hymin*, John 15:4–5). The verb *menō*—"to remain, to dwell"—transfers temple imagery to relationship. It describes neither metaphorical sentiment nor mystical daydream but real spatial communion: shared space between Creator and creature.

Paul's audience, steeped in Jewish imagination, would have heard a familiar echo. The Shekinah—the visible presence of God—once dwelt among Israel in the Tabernacle. Now that same divine presence dwells in the human person. The divine has become personal, the tabernacle portable. The indwelling that once filled a tent now fills a body.

Christ therefore completes the possessive logic of monstrosity but turns it holy. What Sin and Death did as invaders, Christ does as Redeemer. He indwells, animates, speaks through, and transforms, not as parasite, but as presence. The haunted house becomes the living temple (1 Corinthians 3:16–17; 6:14–20; 2 Corinthians 6:14–7:1). Possession becomes participation. The old terror of the monster's voice echoing inside is replaced by the Spirit's whisper: "Abba, Father" (Romans 8:15).

At all three levels—cosmic, human, and indwelling—the Gospel redeems the monstrous. The mythic battle is re-staged as resurrection, the fractured self is healed by divine hybridity, and the parasitic possession of Sin is replaced by the symbiotic indwelling of Christ. What the ancient world feared as monstrosity becomes, in Christian imagination, the very means of salvation.

And from here the argument can only move one way: outward. If Christ is the monster who out-monsters Sin and Death, then every text, myth, and mystery about chaos and order must now bend toward him. What the ancients imagined in symbols of dragon-slaying or descent into the Abyss, he has enacted in flesh and blood. In the next section, we will trace that movement—how the Gospel's crucified hybrid becomes the ultimate chaos-conqueror, the one whose monstrosity is the measure of divine love.

## THE MONSTROUS COMBAT—CHRIST AND THE CHAOS POWERS

From the moment of his incarnation, Jesus enters a world already contested. Scripture never portrays creation as neutral space. It is ordered space—hard-won, upheld by the presence and action of God—and therefore always opposed by powers of dissolution. Israel's poets and prophets spoke of these powers in the symbolic language of the sea, the storm, and the serpent. Leviathan coils beneath the deep (Psalm

74:13–14), the twisting dragon awaits its doom (Isaiah 27:1), and the fleeing serpent must be pierced for life to flourish (Job 26:12–13). These images were not decorative mythology; they were statements about the fragility of order and the God who continually secures it.

Jesus steps directly into that world, not as a neutral observer but as the newest combatant. The Gospels depict him repeatedly confronting the sea—that ancient symbol of chaos—in ways that mark him as the stronger force. When he rebukes the storm (Matthew 8:26), the language is exorcistic. When he walks upon the waves (Matthew 14:25), he treads on the place where monsters dwell. In both scenes, the disciples respond not with applause but with fear—holy fear—because they recognize the pattern: this is the power that subdues the deep. This is the one who does to the sea what God did in the beginning (Genesis 1).

Paul reads these Gospel moments through a broader lens. The ancient *Chaoskampf*—the divine combat against the agents of disorder—now converges upon Christ. The verbs he uses are the old verbs of holy war: Christ "abolished" (*katērgēsē*) the powers (1 Corinthians 15:24), and "Death was swallowed up" (*katapothē*) in victory (15:54), echoing Isaiah 25:8 LXX. What the psalmists once attributed to YHWH's slaying of Leviathan, Paul attributes to the crucified and risen Jesus. The battle is the same, but the combatant is new.

But Paul's most radical move is not assigning Christ the role of divine warrior—Israel had always expected that. The shock is where the battle occurs. "God condemned Sin in the flesh" (Romans 8:3). The *Chaoskampf* shifts from the sea to the body (Gaventa, 2004; 2016; 2024; Käsemann, 1964; 1971; 1994). The monster to be slain is not *out there*, in the deep—it is *in here*, in human flesh, where Sin and Death have taken residence. Christ defeats them not by avoiding embodiment but by entering it, allowing the powers to do their worst so that he might unmake them from the inside. He wins not by evading the monster but by being swallowed by it and detonating life within its gut.

This inversion is the theological heart of the Gospel. Marduk dismembers Tiamat to build a world; Christ permits himself to be dismembered so the world can be built anew. Greek myths picture Zeus overwhelming Typhon from above; Paul pictures Christ descending into Death's domain and overwhelming it from within. The old combat myths imagined gods who kept chaos at arm's length. Paul imagines a God who takes chaos into his own body and burns it out with resurrection life.

The early Christians grasped this. Their Easter hymns speak not merely of victory but of grotesque reversal: Death swallows a victim only to discover divine life tearing it apart from within. Christ is portrayed binding hostile powers and reclaiming what they wrongly claimed. He descends into the depths, forcing open barred realms and exposing the false security of death's dominion itself. His humanity conceals divine force, luring predatory powers to strike, only to have their own violence recoil fatally upon them at last. These images are monstrous, deliberately so. Only a monstrous God defeats monstrous, predatory powers (see Melito of Sardis, *On Pascha*).

For Paul, "He condemned Sin in the flesh" is the final statement of cosmic combat. The courtroom verdict is also the battlefield execution. The flesh, once the monster's dwelling place, becomes the site of the monster's demise. The body of Christ becomes the new stage of the *Chaoskampf*—the definitive slaying of Sin and Death.

This is Christian monstrosity at its clearest: divine power crossing every boundary, entering every realm, embracing every grotesque vulnerability to unmake the monsters that enslave creation. Christ's own flesh becomes the spearpoint of new creation. The chaotic deep has moved inside the human, and Christ has followed it there.

And now, the question becomes: what happens when that same Christ takes up residence in us? What happens when the monster-slayer becomes the indweller?

## THE MONSTROUS GOSPEL—POSSESSION AND RESURRECTION

If Romans 7 describes a haunting and Romans 8 a repossession, then the Gospel itself is the exorcism that makes that exchange permanent. Paul does not conceive salvation as moral upgrade or spiritual encouragement. Salvation is a transfer of tenancy. It is the actual replacement of one indweller with another—the eviction of Sin and Death and the installation of Christ and his Spirit.

John captures this at the macrocosmic level with a single verb: *eskēnōsen*—"to pitch one's tent," "to take up residence." "The Word became flesh and *dwelt among* us" (John 1:14). But Paul pushes it further: the Logos who once "tabernacled" *among us* now dwells *within us* (Romans 8:9–11). The divine habitation moves from the wilderness tent into the human body. Incarnation becomes indwelling.

This is why Jesus once described his own mission in terms of home invasion: "No one can enter the house of the strong man unless he first binds the strong man. Then he may plunder his house" (Mark 3:27). The *ho ischyros/ton ischyron*—the stronger one—is Christ the monster-slayer, breaking into the house that Sin and Death have occupied. Humanity is that house. Our bodies are the stolen goods. The Gospel is the story of Christ binding the intruder and reclaiming his rightful property.

Paul extends this imagery in Colossians 2:15: "He disarmed the rulers and authorities and made a public spectacle of them." The verb *edeigmatisen*—"exposed, displayed"—appears in exorcism texts for naming and humiliating possessing spirits. In other words, the cross is not only execution—it is exposure. Christ names the invaders, binds them, and displays their defeat. The resurrection is their eviction notice served to the cosmos.

This is why the Gospel feels monstrous. It is not gentle advice for troubled souls. It is the violent displacement of illegitimate powers. It overturns tables, bursts tombs, and indwells mortal bodies with immortal life. The Spirit does not hover like sentiment but storms in like a new tenant changing the locks. Every resurrection is an eviction. Every Eucharist is a declaration that the house is under new management.

And this is not confined to humanity. Paul insists creation is haunted, too—groaning under bondage, yearning for liberation (Romans 8:19–23). The Spirit "intercedes" within creation's agony as though pushing new life through the birth canal of decay. Christ's resurrection is the first stage of a cosmic exorcism that will end only when every corner of creation is reoccupied by glory.

The logic is simple but sweeping: indwelling determines destiny. A temple filled with idols becomes an idol's house. A temple filled with glory becomes holy ground. A person filled with Sin and Death behaves like Sin and Death. A person filled with Spirit behaves like resurrection.

If Christ is the monstrous slayer of monsters, and if he now dwells in us, then we are drawn into the same combat. We become not only the battlefield but also the weapon. We become the place where resurrection confronts the powers. We become the extension of his monstrosity in the world.

## THE HOLY MONSTROUS SYMBIOTE

My favorite superhero as a child—and, if I am honest, still today—was Venom. Not Spider-Man, not Captain America, not even the noble figures who stand for order and virtue. It was Venom: the alien symbiote who bonds with a human host, fuses with their body, rearranges their instincts, amplifies their strength, and wages war through them. The appeal of Venom is not merely his power but his paradox: he is both terrifying and transformative. He brings out capacities the host never imagined while simultaneously rewiring the host's life from the inside out.

In the comics, the symbiote first latches onto Spider-Man, merging with him at the cellular level. It mimics his abilities but alters his desires—whispering in his mind, heightening aggression, feeding off his fear, bending his strength toward darker ends. When Peter Parker eventually escapes the symbiote, it seeks a new host in Eddie Brock, fusing with him in a bond that is not possession but something stranger: symbiosis. The two share a nervous system. They speak through one another. They act together. Eddie remains Eddie, but he is now more—stronger, faster, perceptive beyond human limits. The monstrous indweller does not erase him—it weaponizes him.

On screen, the films starring Tom Hardy capture this vividly. When Eddie first bonds with Venom, his body shudders under the weight of a presence not his own. His voice splits—sometimes his, sometimes theirs. His strength surges beyond reason. His hunger shifts. His fear morphs into ferocity. Yet Venom never annihilates Eddie's humanity. Rather, he amplifies it, harnessing Eddie's outrage at injustice, channeling his compassion into violent protection. The symbiote gives Eddie a new capacity for battle because it is fighting its enemies through him. Eddie becomes the battlefield—but also the weapon.

This, of course, is not a perfect analogy for Christ's indwelling. Venom is chaotic, unpredictable, morally ambiguous, and frequently destructive. Christ is none of those things. But as a narrative image—an indwelling power that fuses with the host, empowers the host, and wages its war through the host—it is uncannily fitting for Gospel theology (cf. Gaventa, 2004; 2011; 2016; 2024). If Sin and Death are the monstrous forces inhabiting humanity, then Christ is the holy monster who meets them on their own ground, overwhelms them, and then makes the reclaimed host his own instrument of life.

The New Testament's language of indwelling is not sentimental. Paul speaks of Christ "living in me" (Galatians 2:20), of the Spirit "dwelling in you" (Romans 8:9–11), of believers being "in Christ" and Christ being "in them" in reciprocal habitation. This is not analogy but ontology. What began in Mary's womb continues in every believer: the mingling of divine life with human flesh. The incarnation becomes a template for salvation itself. The God who once took up residence in one human body now takes up residence in many.

In this sense, Christ's indwelling is the anti-symbiote: the inversion of Venom's story. Where Venom amplifies aggression, Christ amplifies compassion. Where Venom feeds on fear, Christ expels it. Where Venom heightens the host's destructive instincts, Christ heightens the host's capacity for self-giving love. But the structure is similar: a presence not the self fuses with the self, energizing the host with a life and power that are both theirs and not theirs. "It is no longer I who live," Paul writes, "but Christ who lives in me" (Galatians 2:20). That is not poetry. It is a description of spiritual symbiosis—holy, healing, and transformative (cf. Fee, 1994).

And just as Venom draws Eddie into battles he could never fight alone, Christ draws believers into the cosmic conflict he himself has already won. We become participants in the ongoing unmaking of Sin and Death. We become extensions of Christ's own monstrosity—his boundary-breaking love, his fearless descent into darkness, his resurrectional defiance of the powers. Through his Spirit, he fights in us, through us, and sometimes despite us. Our bodies become the frontline of the *Chaoskampf*, and our lives become the sites where resurrection energy pushes back against the decay of the world.

But here we reach another paradox that must be named carefully. Christ's monstrosity does not express itself the way monstrous power usually does. His battle is not fought like the wars of the ancient gods, nor like the wars of empires that claim divine sanction. This is not Marduk dismembering Tiamat to establish order through violence, nor Rome "bringing peace" through crucifixion, nor later Christian fantasies of conquering the world for God by force. Christ does not expand his reign by killing enemies or subduing territories. He does not defeat Sin and Death by mirroring their methods. Instead, he exposes and exhausts them. His power is not coercive but invasive, and not violent but revelatory. He unmasks the logic of domination by refusing to participate in it, and in doing so he breaks its hold.

In other words, Christ's war does not look like taking the world back for God. It looks like loving the world to death—and through death—until the powers that feed on fear, violence, and control are left with nothing to consume. Sin and Death rule by accelerating harm, by turning bodies into instruments, by building empires on expendability. Christ dismantles that reign not by out-violencing it, but by absorbing its worst weapons and rendering them useless. The cross is not a tactical failure that precedes victory. It is *the* victory, precisely because it disarms the machinery of domination from the inside. And when Christ indwells his people, he calls them into the same strange resistance—not to extend his kingdom through force, but to live in ways that make the reign of Sin and Death impossible to sustain (Putthoff, 2025a; 2025b; 2025c). His monstrosity spreads wherever violence is refused, enemies are loved, bodies are honored, and life is given rather than taken.

Christ's monstrosity, then, is not grotesque for its own sake but holy for ours. That is to say, he takes what makes monsters monstrous—hybridity, persistence, boundary-crossing—and sanctifies it. He crosses the chasm between divinity and humanity, life and death, heaven and earth, and fuses them in his own person. The very categories that once served as barriers become, in him, the materials of new creation. What was terrifying becomes transformative. What was grotesque becomes glorious.

The incarnation is not a one-time anomaly. It is the beginning of a metamorphosis that now extends into every follower of Christ. The hybrid once feared becomes the hybrid redeemed. The monstrous becomes the means of mercy. The embodied becomes the vessel of the eternal.

Christ's resurrection is therefore not merely his own triumph but the dawn of a new cosmic order. The old invaders—Sin, Death, the powers—still thrash, but their dominion is ending. Their defeat is sealed, their eviction underway. A stronger tenant reigns. As his Spirit spreads, house by house, life by life, creation itself begins to tilt toward restoration. Heaven and earth, long sundered, begin to merge in every body he inhabits.

Which leads naturally to the final movement: if Christ is the holy monster who restores creation by indwelling it, then the Church—his body—is the living continuation of that invasion. We do not merely believe in resurrection; we embody it. The question that remains is whether we will live as hosts of this holy indweller—whether we will let the monster-slayer take residence in our own flesh and make us new.

# CHAPTER 7—CONCLUSION: THE HAUNTED MADE HOLY

## THE STORY RETOLD—FROM HAUNTED TO HOLY

We're now ready to summarize what we've found in the preceding chapters, drawing some conclusions that reshape much of the Gospel story as many of us know it. The story of the Bible is not a fall from innocence but a struggle for habitation. From its opening line—"and the Spirit of God was hovering over the waters"—Scripture has been a story about presence: who dwells where, and who belongs in the house of creation (Terrien, 1978). Humanity, formed of dust and filled with divine breath, was never meant to live apart from God's indwelling. The human body itself was created as sacred space, the first temple in which heaven and earth met. To be human was to be inhabited—to bear the divine presence as the life within our clay (Putthoff, 2020).

But that habitation was broken. Sin and Death, those ancient squatters, entered the story not as metaphors for bad behavior but as living powers. Like invasive species, they found their way into the ecosystem of creation and began to spread. They colonized bodies and institutions, minds and empires. What began as a temple became a haunted house. God's likeness in the human self was not erased, but it was obscured, shrouded by rival presences that claimed his dwelling for themselves.

From that moment forward, the drama of Scripture is not about moral failure or divine disappointment. It is about displacement and return. God's mission is not merely to forgive us but to move back in—to reclaim his world from the powers that invaded it. That is what makes the Gospel good news. It is not the announcement of a pardon but the declaration of repossession. When Christ enters the world, he comes not as a lawyer to negotiate our innocence but as the stronger one who storms the house, binds the captors, and reclaims what is his. The incarnation is the invasion of the divine landlord. The resurrection is his eviction notice to Death itself.

This is why the Gospel cannot be reduced to guilt and pardon. Guilt is a symptom, not the disease, and forgiveness is a doorway, not the destination. The real story is habitation—the divine taking up residence again in human flesh and in the world itself. Christ is God's return to his temple. The Spirit is the settling of his presence into the rooms we thought too defiled to be holy. We are not criminals awaiting acquittal but sacred ruins being restored. The haunted are being made holy.

## THE SELF AS TEMPLE, THE WORLD AS BATTLEFIELD

Paul's vision of humanity unfolds within this very drama. He does not see the self as a moral ledger, balancing good and bad deeds, but as sacred architecture—a structure built of dust, designed for breath. Yet that architecture has been breached. "It is no longer I who do it," Paul writes, "but Sin dwelling in me." That sentence is not confession; it is diagnosis (Gaventa, 2004; 2024; Käsemann, 1994; Dunn, 1988; 1998). The human problem is not willpower but occupancy. We are not bad people trying to be good. Rather, we are living temples invaded by powers we cannot expel on our own.

Romans 7 names this invasion, and Romans 8 narrates its reversal (Jewett, 2007; Gaventa, 2004; 2016; 2024). In chapter 7, Sin and Death take up residence. In chapter 8, the Spirit reclaims the house. And this, Paul insists, is not only a personal reality—it is a cosmic one. What is true of the body is true of the world. Creation itself is a desecrated temple under reconstruction (Wright, 2013). Its earthquakes and extinctions, its beauty and its pain, are not signs of meaninglessness but of renovation. Paul says the whole creation "groans in labor pains," awaiting the full revelation of God's children (Romans 8:22). The Spirit who breathes in us breathes through galaxies. Every tremor, every groan, is the sound of a cosmos being repossessed. The temple of the world is being cleansed, and the glory is returning to fill it.

The self, then, is both temple and battlefield—an interior holy place under siege, where the powers of Sin and the presence of the Spirit contend for habitation. This is not a metaphor for inner conflict. It is a metaphysical reality. The war of gods has moved inside the human. But unlike the myths of the ancient world, this war will not end in chaos. The Spirit is stronger. The renovation has already begun. And though the walls still bear the scars of occupation, the light through the cracks tells us that God is home again.

## THE GOSPEL AS EXORCISM AND RESURRECTION

The Gospel, therefore, is not advice for self-improvement or therapy for the guilty conscience. It is the exorcism of creation. It is the story of God reclaiming his world from the squatters of Sin and Death. The cross is not a metaphorical sacrifice offered by God in which God himself is appeasing his own wrath at otherwise decent people. Far from it, the cross is a strategic infiltration of enemy territory. Christ enters the realm of Death deliberately, the way light enters a tomb, to unmake it from within. The resurrection is not escape—it is expulsion. Death itself is driven out of the body it once ruled. Christ's resurrection is an eviction notice served to Death.

This is why the Gospel first feels disruptive before it feels comforting. Exorcisms always do. Liberation is rarely neat work. When the Spirit takes possession of a life, there is shaking, groaning, resistance. Old voices rise up in protest. But they are being silenced. When Paul declares, "There is therefore now no condemnation for those who are in Christ Jesus," he is not soothing guilty consciences. He is instead announcing that the courtroom has been overruled. The entire system of accusation and shame—the empire of condemnation—has been abolished. The verdict is thus not "innocent." It is "inhabited."

Forgiveness is only the doorway. Habitation is the goal. To be Christian is not merely to be pardoned but to be possessed by the Spirit who raised Jesus from the dead. The cross was the battle, the resurrection the cleansing, and Pentecost the moving day. The haunted world has not been abandoned—it is being reoccupied, room by room, heart by heart. The Spirit now breathes in places long thought lost, animating both flesh and soil, turning haunted matter into holy ground.

That is the Gospel: God has come home. Immanuel is here to stay.

## SOME PEOPLE REALLY ARE HARMFUL

There is a question that inevitably rises whenever we begin speaking about Sin and Death as invading powers rather than as private moral failures: What about people who are actually terrible? Not people who wrestle with addiction or trauma, not those living with wounds they don't know how to carry, not those whose lives collapse under the weight of grief or mental anguish. I mean people who genuinely harm others—people who weaponize their agency, who exploit, abuse, coerce, or manipulate. Are they simply victims of Sin, too? Does this framework excuse their behavior? Do they get to shrug off harm because "Sin lives in me, not I"? In other words: are truly bad people responsible for the evil they choose to do?

The short answer is yes. The long answer is that the Bible itself insists upon it—perhaps surprisingly to many—far more explicitly and consistently than most Christians probably realize.

The modern notion that "all sin is equal" is not only absent in Scripture, but it is directly contradicted by Scripture. The biblical story assumes a hierarchy of harm. But Scripture differentiates sharply, relentlessly, between personal frailty and predatory behavior, between internal struggle and external destruction, between wounds we carry and wounds we inflict. No biblical prophet, psalmist, apostle, or even Jesus himself, ever collapses all wrongdoing into one flat category. In fact, the Bible's moral imagination is built around the exact opposite premise: that harm done to others is categorically different from moral struggles that harm only oneself.

This is why the prophets direct nearly every oracle of judgment toward the *powerful*, not the *weak*, and toward those who gain power and wealth at the expense of those who cannot defend themselves. When Isaiah thunders on behalf of God, he doesn't accuse ordinary people of having lustful thoughts or struggling with insecurity. Far from it—he goes after the leaders, legislators, and landowners who "make unjust decrees" and "rob the poor of their rights" (Isaiah 10:1–2). Micah doesn't condemn the anxious or the addicted. Quite contrarily, he condemns those who "covet fields and seize them," who "defraud a man of his home" (Micah 2:1–2). Amos calls down fire not on teenagers making bad choices, but on elites who "trample the poor into the dust of the earth" and "profit from dishonest scales" (Amos 2:6–7; 8:4–6). Ezekiel and Micah reserve their harshest words for leaders who eat the flesh of God's people (Micah 3:3) and tear them apart like wolves (Ezekiel 22:27). The psalms echo these, crying out for deliverance from the violent, the arrogant, the oppressor (cf. Psalms 10, 37, and 73).

Across the entirety of the Hebrew Bible, or Old Testament, God's condemnation is *consistently aimed at people who harm others*—and at the social, religious, economic, and political systems such people build to protect and continue that harm—not at those who are victims of bad people, even if those victims do commit their own sins.

Jesus stands firmly in this prophetic line. Contrary to popular imagination, Jesus does not reserve his fiercest warnings for the sinful, the broken, or the morally confused. He reserves them for predators— especially religious, economic, and political predators. His "woes" in Matthew 23 are laser-focused on the scribes and Pharisees who use religious authority to crush the vulnerable. He accuses them of "devouring widows' houses" (Mark 12:40), exploiting the desperate while appearing righteous. His parables of judgment, including the famous one in Matthew 25, do not condemn struggling sinners—they condemn those who ignored the hungry, the imprisoned, the stranger, the sick. In Jesus' world, judgment is not about failing to meet religious standards. It is about refusing to meet human need.

Paul carries this thread forward. When the apostle warns that "the unrighteous will not inherit the Kingdom of God" (1 Corinthians 6:9–10), he does not list regular human failings, but he specifically lists actions that destroy communities: greed, violence, exploitation, theft, abuse, deception. These are relational, structural, outwardly harmful forms of wrongdoing. Likewise, when Paul warns about "the works of the flesh" (Galatians 5:19–21), the majority of these items describe patterns of relational harm—enmity, jealousy, fits of rage, rivalries, dissensions, factions, envy. Paul's vision of judgment targets those who participate in the powers in such a way that they spread destruction, not those who carry private pain, sin along the way, and feel guilt and shame day and night.

Revelation brings this distinction into cosmic focus. Its judgments are directed at violent empire (Revelation 13, 17, 18), economic exploitation (Revelation 18:11–13), corrupt leadership, persecutors of the saints (Revelation 6:9–11), and systems that profit from death. Revelation's imagery is so vivid and frightening precisely because it is aimed at those who wield their influence like a weapon. It's not aimed at those of us who genuinely want to follow Jesus and behave better but who fall short of our goals.

In every corner of Scripture—Torah, Prophets, Wisdom literature, Gospels, Epistles, Apocalypse—the same pattern holds true: God is relentlessly on the side of the oppressed, and he is relentlessly opposed to the oppressor.

So back to the question: are there actually bad people? The Bible's answer is, unequivocally, yes. But this is not because some people are born worse than others. It is because some people choose—habitually, persistently, over the course of their lives—to align themselves with the powers of Sin and Death that inhabit their members and to live in ways that harm human beings. And Scripture holds such people responsible.

The framework I've offered in this book—that the human self is a temple, a dwelling place contested by rival powers—does not absolve anyone of responsibility. It actually heightens it, especially for those who seek to benefit themselves by harming others. If our bodies can host Sin and Death not only in internal temptation but in externally destructive action, then our choices matter profoundly. We become morally responsible not merely for our internal condition but for what we allow to live through us. When someone cooperates with the powers in ways that harm others, they become complicit in the cosmic invasion. And Scripture insists that they will be confronted for it.

To say that Sin and Death are real powers is not to excuse human harm. It is to explain how human beings become conduits for that harm. It is to diagnose the process by which a person can gradually hand over the rooms of the self to a predatory tenant until they become, in biblical terms, "full of violence" (Genesis 6:11), or "given over" (Romans 1:24–28), or aligned with "the beast" (Revelation 13). In these moments, the human is not replaced, but the human is certainly corrupted—and it is judged not as a puppet but as a partner.

This means that divine judgment, far from being a cosmic overreaction, is an act of cosmic protection. Judgment is God shutting down the human branch offices of Sin and Death. It is God defending the humans whom harm has devoured. It is God insisting that predators cannot reign forever, that wounded people will not be swallowed whole. Judgment is a profound act of mercy—not for the perpetrator, but for the victim. It is God's refusal to let the monsters keep feasting on defenseless human prey.

So, yes, some people genuinely become bad—not in the shame-based sense of being "dirty" or "unworthy," but in the relational sense of becoming complicit in the destruction of others. And yes, Scripture holds them responsible. You cannot outsource cruelty to Sin. You cannot blame your violence on the invader. As Paul says, "Do not let Sin reign in your mortal body... do not present your members to Sin" (*mē oun basileuetō hē hamartia en tō thnētō hymōn sōmati... mēde paristanete ta melē hymōn hopla adikias tē hamartia*, Romans 6:12–13). Here, Paul's imperative assumes agency. It assumes responsibility. It assumes that choices shape habitation.

Even Isaiah's frightening description of Sheol indicates that it's not just anyone who should fear the bloodthirsty Abyss, but specifically those who use their power and wealth to harm and oppress others.

> Therefore, Sheol has enlarged (*hirḥībāh*) its appetite and opened its mouth without measure (*ūfaʿărāh pīhā livlī-ḥōq*); and Jerusalem's nobility, her multitude, her din of revelry, and her jubilant throng shall go down into it (Isaiah 5:14).

It's almost as if Sheol—like Leviathan and Behemoth, or even Satan— serve as tools in the hands of God if or when he sees fit to call them into service. Here, Sheol swallows and devours in terrifying fashion. But it devours specifically those who enjoy a life of luxury at the expense of others.

The good news of the Gospel, then, is not that God overlooks such harm. It's that he is stronger than it. It's that his judgment is aimed not at vulnerable "sinners" but at the predators, exploiters, and systems that destroy human life. Divine judgment is not the opposite of divine love. It is love protecting the beloved.

## WHAT ABOUT ORIGINAL SIN? HOW BEHAVIOR TRANSFORMS

Because the doctrine of "original sin" has dominated Western Christianity for so long, it is impossible to talk about Sin and Death as invading powers without addressing it honestly. Most Christians today—whether Catholic, Protestant, evangelical, or even loosely Christian—inherit a theological reflex that traces back to Augustine. In *Contra Julian* and *On the Merits and Forgiveness of Sins*, Augustine argued that Adam's sin corrupted human nature itself, leaving every human being born guilty, internally depraved, and morally incapable of choosing good apart from divine intervention. Medieval theology amplified this. Luther inherited it, insisting in a phrase picked up by Karl Barth (*CD* IV), that humanity is "curved in on itself" (*incurvatus in se*) from birth (*LW* 25). Calvin systematized this idea into the doctrine of "total depravity," arguing in the *Institutes* (II.1–3) that every faculty of human nature is corrupted from conception.

This is the air many Christians still breathe. It shapes evangelism ("you're born a sinner"), preaching ("your nature is wicked"), and even pastoral care or parental messaging ("your heart is deceitful," or even "your child is wicked, and that's why they misbehave"), misinterpreted as a universal anthropology. However, this is not how Scripture itself describes the human condition, nor is it how Paul uses Adam or speaks of the self. Paul never actually says humans inherit guilt from Adam. His emphasis is inherited environment.

"Sin entered the world," Paul writes, "and Death through Sin, and so Death spread to all humanity" (Romans 5:12). Death spreads like a contagion, not guilt like a courtroom sentence. Paul's language is ecological, not legal. Adam opens a door in the ecosystem of creation, and through that opening, predatory forces seep into the world. Those forces—Sin (as a power), Death (as a ruler)—alter the environment into which humans are born. We are not born depraved, but we are born invaded.

This is important, because if babies are born guilty, then human agency doesn't matter at all. But if humans are born into a world already haunted, then agency matters immensely. Vulnerability is not the same as depravity.

Paul makes this distinction a number of times. In Ephesians 2:2, he describes humanity as walking "according to the ruler of the power of the air," meaning that humans drift with the currents of a corrupted atmosphere—not because they are evil by nature, but because they inhale what surrounds them. In 1 Corinthians 15:22, Paul writes, "In Adam all die," not "In Adam all are guilty." The consequence is mortality, not moral condemnation.

But if we are not born corrupted, then how do we become capable of evil? Paul's answer is straightforward and frightening: we become like the powers we repeatedly cooperate with. Behavior is not superficial. As a technology of the self, human action is the mechanism of metamorphosis (Foucault, 1988; Putthoff, 2017). As Paul says in Romans 6:12, "Do not let Sin reign in your mortal body," and in 6:13, "Do not present your members to Sin as instruments for unrighteousness." Notice the verbs: let, present. They assume choice. Sin gains territory by invitation, not essence.

In Romans 7:17 and 7:20, Paul speaks of "Sin dwelling in me," using the verb *oikeō*—to inhabit, to reside. This is habitation, not inherent nature. And in Romans 8, he switches the occupant: "The Spirit of God dwells (*oikei*) in you" (Romans 8:9, 11). For Paul, the human self is porous, permeable, capable of hosting rival presences. The question, therefore, is not, "What is my nature?" but, "Who is my tenant?"

This Gospel also reframes behavior. Behaviors are not mere moral actions. They are acts of alignment. In Romans 8:4–13, when Paul contrasts "walking according to the flesh" with "walking according to the Spirit," he is not contrasting body vs. soul. "Flesh" (*sarx*) is shorthand for the sphere ruled by Sin and Death—the invaded ecosystem (see Käsemann, 1964; 1969; 1971). To "walk according to the flesh" (Romans 8:4) is to move in step with those occupying powers. To "set the mind on the flesh" (Romans 8:6) is to tune one's inner world to their voice. To "put to death the deeds of the body by the Spirit" (Romans 8:13) is to resist those powers through cooperation with the indwelling God.

Paul's vision here is deeply behavioral and deeply spiritual. We become what we repeatedly give ourselves to. Romans 1 describes this same metamorphosis negatively. Three times Paul says, "God gave them over"—using the verb *paradidōmi*—in Romans 1:24, 26, and 28. This does not describe God sentencing people to eternal damnation, but God allowing them to experience the consequences of their chosen patterns of allegiance. Their behaviors—idolatry, exploitation,

136

violence, envy, deceit, ruthlessness—reshape them into creatures that mirror the powers they serve. These are not private sins, either, but they are socially destructive patterns (Romans 1:29–31). Paul is not diagnosing inherited depravity but progressive deformation through repeated alignment with Sin and Death. And crucially, he is not lumping private, internal struggles into the same category as these outwardly harmful, socially destructive behaviors. The two categories of conduct are not the same, and Scripture—and God—does not treat them the same.

Galatians 5 echoes this. The "works of the flesh" (Galatians 5:19–21) are overwhelmingly relational harms—enmity, strife, jealousy, fits of rage, dissensions, factions, envy. Conversely, the "fruit of the Spirit" (*ho de karpos tou pneumatos*, Galatians 5:22–23) emerges not because God overrides human nature but because humans cooperate with the divine presence. Here, again, the behavior Paul is addressing is behavior that harms others—not the private, internal struggles that generate shame or fear but do not destroy another's life.

Ephesians 4:22–24 describes this as "putting off the old humanity" (*apothesthai … ton palaion anthrōpon*) and "putting on the new" (*endysasthai ton kainon anthrōpon*). This is not a passive state but an active re-habituation—the slow retraining of desires, instincts, and patterns of response. And here, too, Paul ties the transformation directly to behavior. The old humanity is "corrupted according to deceitful desires" (*phtheiromenon kata tas epithymias tēs apatēs*), while the new humanity is "created according to God in righteousness and holiness in truth" (*ton kata theon ktisthenta en dikaiosynē kai hosiotēti tēs alētheias*). In other words, Paul insists that the interior renovation of the self happens through embodied choices. Our behaviors either reinforce the old patterns of the invaded world or cooperate with the new patterns of the indwelling Spirit.

This is why early Judaism never taught Augustine's idea of inherited guilt. This is why many streams of early Judaism did not frame the problem the way Augustine would—as inherited guilt—and instead spoke in terms of competing inclinations. Human beings were believed to have two inclinations—the *yēṣer hā-rāʿ* (desire that can go wrong) and the *yēṣer ha-ṭōb* (desire toward good). Not depraved, not pristine—capable of either, shaped by environment, community, and habit. Paul, standing within that world, radicalizes the concept, insisting that human inclinations are not just internal but invasive. And the solution is not moral improvement. It's not simply acting better. But it's about a new inhabitation.

This also redefines sanctification. Instead of becoming more moral through effort, we become more Spirit-saturated through cooperation. Instead of perfectionism, the Gospel is about participation. Instead of managing *sin*, it is about evicting *Sin*.

The change is gradual, cellular, systemic, in Paul's imagination. Humans are not inherently depraved, but we are inherently porous. We become what we allow to inhabit us. The more we obey Sin and Death, the more like it we become. But the more we obey the Spirit, by virtue of its living presence inside of us, the more like it, like God and Christ, we become.

This also explains why some people become morally monstrous. Not because God created them that way, and not because Adam's guilt corrupted their essence, but because they consistently present their bodies as "instruments of unrighteousness" (*hopla adikias*, Romans 6:13). As Paul puts it, they "present their members" (*paristanete ta melē hymōn*) to Sin, handing over their capacities, desires, and embodied agency to a power eager to occupy whatever space it is given. They cooperate with the invader until it reshapes them from the inside.

And it explains why others become saints—not because they were born righteous, but because they repeatedly open themselves to the Spirit. They cooperate with divine life until their instincts, habits, perceptions, and desires become aligned with God's own.

So Paul's anthropology is not "sin nature" but habitation, alignment, and metamorphosis. It's not about original guilt—it's instead about original vulnerability. It's also not about some vaguely defined, non-biblical inherited depravity—it's about inherited occupation. We are born into a world where two powers compete for dwelling space. And we become the creature of the one we host, the one we obey.

## THE DIVINE MONSTER AND THE NEW HUMANITY

If Sin and Death are the monsters that devour, Christ is the monstrous love that devours the devourers. He is the holy transgressor who crosses every boundary that Sin and Death built to keep God and creation apart. In him, divinity and dust meet without confusion and without division. He breaks the categories that once defined both gods and mortals, revealing that the deepest holiness is not distance but incarnation. His life is the paradox of divine monstrosity: terrifying to the powers that ruled the world, yet healing to the world they ruled.

The cross is the ultimate manifestation of that holy monstrosity. To Rome, it was blasphemy and shame, and to the evil powers, it was devastation. The divine should not bleed, and the immortal should not die—but Christ does both, and in doing so, he overturns the logic of heaven and hell alike. He enters the Abyss not as victim but as invader, consuming Death from within. The monsters of the old order—those hybrid gods of chaos and corruption—are confronted by one who is both more human and more divine than they can comprehend. The Creator has joined the creation, and the creature who once bore his likeness now bears his Spirit.

This is why the Gospel always moves from Christ to Christ in you. Salvation is not admiration at a distance but participation in Christ's being. The one who is both God and human has made humanity the site of divine life. "If anyone is in Christ: they are a new type of creature" (2 Corinthians 5:17). The phrase does not describe a moral upgrade but a cosmic rebirth. The same creative power that hovered over the waters in Genesis now breathes through human lungs. The resurrection of Jesus is not only his vindication—it is the prototype of ours. His indwelling Spirit reconstitutes the human as a new kind of hybrid: dust still, yet burning with divine fire.

Athanasius captured this paradox when he wrote, "The Son of God became human so that humanity might become divine" (*CCC* 460). He was not speaking of self-deification but of participation—the sharing of divine life through indwelling Spirit. The incarnation did not end with Christ's ascension—it multiplied. The body of Christ expanded into the bodies of believers, so that what was once monstrous—God in flesh— became the norm of new creation. The scandal of the incarnation becomes the structure of salvation.

This redefines holiness. It is no longer separation from matter but the saturation of matter with God's life. To be holy is not to escape the world but to embody God within it. It is to stand, as Christ did, in the liminal space between heaven and earth and to hold them together. It is to walk into tombs and find them empty, to touch what others call unclean and call it beloved, to cross every border that fear has built. The holy person, in Paul's imagination, is not a recluse but a re-creator— one through whom the Spirit continues Christ's work of reclamation.

Holiness, then, is not fragility but fearlessness. It is resurrectional courage—the refusal to be defined by decay, despair, or death. The saints are those who live as if resurrection were already underway because, in them, it is. They are not moral paragons or flawless heroes; they are living proof that divine life can dwell in mortal clay. The new humanity is not perfect, but possessed—its breath synced with the Spirit's, its body animated by the same life that raised Jesus from the dead.

In this sense, the "divine monster" now becomes the template for redeemed humanity. We too are hybrid beings—born of dust, filled with divinity. What once made us vulnerable to possession now makes us capable of communion. The liminality that once invited the invader now welcomes the indweller. In Christ, the monstrous has become holy, the hybrid healed. The world's most scandalous truth remains its deepest hope: that God still refuses to stay in heaven, and that the human body—fragile, fearful, finite—is still the place he chooses to call home.

## THE POETIC VICTORY—THE DEATH OF DEATH

Paul's Gospel ends not with an argument but with a taunt. "The last enemy to be destroyed is Death," he writes, before turning and mocking it to its face: "Where, O Death, is your victory? Where, O Death, is your sting?" (1 Corinthians 15:26, 55).

Only someone who has seen Death unmade can speak like that. Paul glimpsed a world already under new management, a cosmos where the great devourer had choked on life itself. For him, resurrection was not the postponement of Death but its undoing—the swallowing of the swallower. Death remains visible, but only as a hollowed shell of its former self, a broken parasite still pretending to reign.

Centuries later, John Donne caught the same defiant spirit and gave it melody. His *Holy Sonnet X* (c. 1609–1610) is not pious consolation but sacred mockery—the laughter of one who knows that the grave has already been emptied of its power:

*Death be not proud, though some have called thee*
*Mighty and dreadful, for thou art not so;*
*For those whom thou think'st thou dost overthrow*
*Die not, poor Death, nor yet canst thou kill me.*
*From rest and sleep, which but thy pictures be,*
*Much pleasure; then from thee much more must flow,*
*And soonest our best men with thee do go—*
*Rest of their bones, and soul's delivery.*
*Thou art slave to fate, chance, kings, and desperate men,*
*And dost with poison, war, and sickness dwell;*
*And poppy or charms can make us sleep as well*
*And better than thy stroke. Why swell'st thou then?*
*One short sleep past, we wake eternally,*
*And Death shall be no more; Death, thou shalt die.*

Donne's poem does what Paul's letters do—it personifies Death only to strip it bare. Naming the monster is the first act of exorcism. Once exposed, it can no longer rule by fear. To mock Death is not to deny it but to place it within the Gospel's logic of reversal: that everything Death touches, God will raise, and everything it consumes, Christ will reclaim.

This is the laughter of God at the grave—the cosmic irony that the instrument of humiliation became the weapon of triumph. The cross was Death's greatest victory until it turned out to be its final defeat. In crucifying the Lord of life, Death impaled itself upon its own dominion. The resurrection is the punchline of that divine joke, the moment when all of creation hears God's laughter echo through the tomb.

And yet the victory is not only Christ's. Paul insists that it is ours as well. The same Spirit who raised Jesus now inhabits us (Romans 8:11). Every breath drawn in that Spirit is a protest against Death's pretense, a small resurrection in advance. Every act of love, every gesture of forgiveness, every courage that refuses despair is resurrectional resistance—the life of the stronger one continuing his work through the haunted now made holy.

So the Gospel ends where it began, with God in the flesh, breath in dust, life in the midst of what once was dead. The desecrated temple has been cleansed, the house of the world has been repossessed, and what began as a haunting ends in habitation. This is the story worth retelling: that Sin and Death are not metaphors but monsters, that Christ is the stronger one who has bound them, and that his Spirit now dwells in the house they once defiled.

The haunted world is being made holy again—and even Death shall die. That is the Gospel. Thanks be to God for it.

# EPILOGUE—WHAT ALL OF THIS MEANS: GOSPEL, NOT SHAME

I've spent this book tracing ancient myths, monstrous powers, and the strange, brilliant theology of Scripture, focusing especially on Paul's letters. We've wandered through Babylon and the Galilee, through the ruins of Leviathan and the shadow of the cross. But now I want to speak plainly—about what all of this really means.

For many of us, the Gospel we've been taught is a courtroom story. God is the judge, we are the guilty defendants, and Jesus steps in to take our punishment so that we can be acquitted.

That story can stir repentance and gratitude—but it's not the full story. It shrinks the vast cosmic drama of Scripture into a single legal metaphor. It makes the Gospel about what we've done wrong instead of what God is doing right now.

The word Gospel itself—*euangelion* in Greek—literally means "good news." In the ancient world, it wasn't a religious term but a political one. A "gospel" was the royal announcement of victory: the proclamation that an enemy had been defeated, captives freed, and a new king enthroned. When Mark opens his story with, "The beginning of the Gospel of Jesus Christ, the Son of God" (Mark 1:1), he's echoing the language of imperial decrees. Jesus has arrived, Mark declares, and he's in the process of reclaiming his rightful place on the throne of the cosmos. Paul uses "gospel" the same way, as a declaration that Sin and Death have lost their power and that Christ now reigns (Romans 1:1–4; 1 Corinthians 15:24–26). The Gospel, then, is not advice about how to behave better or a summons to guilt—it is the cosmic announcement that the tyrants have fallen, the prisoners are being set free, and the true ruler has taken the throne.

Contrary to the way you've probably been taught—or even taught others yourself—there is no room in ancient ideas about the "gospel" (*euangelion*) for shame, guilt, or fear. Gospel is, by its very nature, the opposite of that—it's the removal of shame, guilt, or fear. It's the new Lord, new King, new Savior breaking into enemy territory, defeating the occupiers, destroying their strongholds, and dismantling their powers. If someone begins the story of the Gospel with anything but this, they have missed the point entirely.

Paul's Gospel is just that: Good News. It is not a courtroom story in which you are on trial. It's a house story in which God has returned to rescue you. It's about who lives where—who inhabits creation, and who inhabits us. The Bible's story begins with God's Spirit breathing into dust, filling matter with divine life. Humanity was never meant to be "good enough" for God. Humanity was meant to be inhabited by God. Sin and Death didn't make us bad people—they made us homeless. They broke the connection between breath and dust, between Creator and creature.

That's what Jesus came to restore. He didn't come as a heavenly accountant to adjust the balance sheet of guilt and innocence. He came as the Stronger One who storms the haunted house, binds the captors, and moves back in. The cross was not God's anger at humanity satisfied but his presence returning to his beloved. And the resurrection was not escape from the world but God's re-entry into it. Pentecost, then, was not a symbol—it was a move-in day. The Gospel has therefore never been about guilt and pardon, but it's always been about habitation and liberation.

This means that you are not primarily a criminal needing acquittal. You are a temple under restoration. You are a sacred space being reclaimed. The Spirit is not your parole officer but your tenant and your life. Read within this framework, the story of the Bible is not a fall from innocence but a struggle for habitation—a long battle over who lives in the house God built.

And yes, we still mess up. We still commit "sins." But those moments do not mean Sin (the capital-S tyrant) has reclaimed you. They are echoes, not ownership. Think of them as the last whispers of the old tenant trying to rattle the pipes and scare you into believing he's still in charge. Every act of cruelty, greed, or fear feeds that echo, while every act of mercy, love, and justice strengthens the Spirit's presence. This isn't moralism—it's metaphysics. Each action aligns you with one indweller or the other, either Spirit or Sin.

So, Christian discipline isn't about earning forgiveness. It's about cooperation with the renovation. Repentance is not self-loathing—it's re-alignment. Prayer, community, and confession aren't ways to make God love you. Rather, they're ways to open more rooms to His presence. Over time, the old wallpaper of shame peels away, and the light begins to fill every corner.

If you take nothing else from this book, remember this: the Gospel is not merely God's pardon of the guilty. It is God's repossession of the haunted. It is not about you proving yourself worthy to an angry God but instead about God proving that he will not leave his creation behind. Nor is it a story of sin management. After all, you are not defined by your failures. You are defined by who lives in you. The Spirit's indwelling means the old powers have no deed, no lease, no right of return. Shame has no standing here, and you are not the problem God came to solve. You are the temple God came to reclaim.

And that should change everything about the way you see God, Sin, Death, and yourself. It means the Gospel is not an emergency measure— it's the restoration of God's original dream. It means the Christian life is not a project of sin avoidance but of divine participation. It means that even in our weakness, even in our confusion, the stronger one lives inside us—and He is still at work making all things new.

This is what Paul meant when he said, "Christ in you, the hope of glory." So, here it is—this is the Gospel: glory, not guilt. Indwelling, not shame. Freedom, not fear.

You are haunted, yes—but by the Spirit who raised the world from Chaos.

You are possessed, yes—but by the loving God who spoke creation into being.

And that God, who lives inside you, will never let you go.

# APPENDIX—RESITUATING SATAN IN THE BIBLICAL DRAMA

## WHAT ABOUT THE DEVIL?

Most of us inherit a version of the devil that feels ancient and biblical, but that picture has been shaped far more by medieval imagination, Dante and Milton, and centuries of preaching than by the biblical texts themselves. In this inherited narrative, Satan is God's great rival: he was a glorious angel named Lucifer who rebelled, was cast out of heaven, and now rules demons from a fiery underworld. He presides over hell like a dark emperor, orchestrates temptation on earth and eternal punishment below. Some of this development comes from Second Temple Jewish literature and early Christian interpretation as well, but medieval and early modern imagination gave it the shape most people now assume. It is certainly a compelling story, and it has supplied the architecture for much of Western Christian imagination. But when we turn back to Scripture, that portrait becomes harder to sustain. The devil of the Bible is real, but he is not the figure of popular Christian mythology.

### The Origins of Ha-Sāṭān, the Accuser

The Hebrew Bible's portrayal of "the satan" is a good place to start. The word satan is not a personal name but a title—the adversary, the accuser. In Job 1–2, *ha-sāṭān* appears not on the margins of creation but inside the divine council, moving freely among the "sons of God" and presenting himself before YHWH. His role is prosecutorial: he questions God's evaluation of Job's integrity and asks permission to test him. Far from ruling a kingdom of darkness, he operates as a kind of celestial attorney whose authority is derivative and whose actions require divine consent. Something similar happens in Zechariah 3:1–2, where the satan stands to accuse the high priest Joshua until the Lord rebukes him. In these early appearances, the adversary is neither God's equal nor his opposite. He is a subordinate agent whose job is to test, accuse, and probe the boundaries of human righteousness.

### The Shift from the Accuser to the Agent of Judgment

Only later does the term begin to move toward a more personal identity. In 1 Chronicles 21:1, "Satan stood up against Israel and incited David to take a census." But even this is complicated by the earlier parallel in 2 Samuel 24:1, where it is God who incites David. The Chronicler reframes the agency, but he does not suddenly introduce a cosmic anti-God. Instead, he takes an ambiguous divine action and assigns it to an adversarial figure. The satan becomes a convenient way of speaking about divine judgment without attributing destructive agency directly to God. Even here, however, his role is limited: he influences, provokes, tests—but he does not reign.

### Emerging Conceptions of the Adversary Figure

The intertestamental period expanded the devil's profile by drawing together older adversary traditions with the myth of the fallen Watchers (*1 Enoch* 6–11). Yet even here, evil remains decentralized. The world is populated by multiple spirits, wandering demons, and rebellious beings, but no single figure emerges as the sovereign of evil. Satan becomes more recognizable as a character, but he is still not the supreme opposite of God. He moves within a crowded supernatural landscape and operates as one figure among many.

### The Personal Tempter in the Gospels

By Jesus' day, the satan figure has sharpened into a personal tempter, yet the New Testament continues to resist the idea that he is God's great rival. In the wilderness temptation narratives (Matthew 4:1–11; Luke 4:1–13), Satan engages Jesus in theological debate. He quotes Scripture accurately but applies it deceitfully. His offer of "all the kingdoms of the world" (Matthew 4:8–9) reveals the extent of his influence, but even this authority is derivative. He is not creating kingdoms but simply leveraging the political structures of a world already in disarray. His tactics are rhetorical, not ontological. He manipulates rather than commands. He proposes rather than compels. And when Jesus resists him, Satan simply departs "until an opportune time" (Luke 4:13). The devil is dangerous, but he is not sovereign.

In the Gospels as a whole, Satan rarely acts directly. He "enters" Judas (Luke 22:3), but this is both possession in the horror-movie sense and the exploitation of Judas's existing weakness. He "demands to sift" Peter (Luke 22:31), but he cannot act without divine permission. Most of his activity in the Gospels and Acts is mediated through deception, accusation, and manipulation. The devil's power is real, but it is power through persuasion—power through distortion. Jesus calls him "a liar and the father of lies" (John 8:44). His native language is deception. When the New Testament attributes influence to Satan, it usually refers to his ability to distort truth rather than his ability to dominate the cosmos.

## The Opportunistic Diplomat of the Powers

Paul's letters continue this pattern of muted but realistic portrayal. Paul rarely talks about Satan, and when he does (e.g., 1 Thessalonians 2:18; 2 Corinthians 2:11), the devil is an opportunist who hinders, blinds, or deceives. Paul gives him influence but not sovereignty. He never attributes human enslavement primarily to Satan. Paul reserves the role of enslaver for Sin and Death. Those powers, not the devil, are the ones who "reign," "rule," "enslave," and "dwell within" human bodies (Romans 5–7). Satan is a strategist of deception, but he is not the tyrant of the human condition. The real tyrants in Paul's worldview are the powers that occupy human flesh and corrupt the human will.

## From Prosecutor to Parasite

Revelation gives Satan his most dramatic portrayal, merging the ancient serpent of Genesis with the dragon imagery of Leviathan (Revelation 12:9). He deceives the nations, empowers the beast, wages war on the saints, and tries to devour the messianic child. Yet even in Revelation, he is not the final enemy destroyed. The climactic forces thrown into the lake of fire at the end of the book are Death and Hades (Revelation 20:14). Satan had already been bound, released, defeated, and thrown down (v. 10)—but the last enemy to fall is Death itself. Revelation preserves Satan's mythic importance but does not elevate him to cosmic primacy. His power is significant, but it is not ultimate.

## The Devil We Don't Recognize

Taken together, the biblical portrait of Satan is surprisingly restrained. The devil is a nuisance, tempter, accuser, opportunist, and deceiver. He manipulates systems, distorts truth, and weaponizes human weakness. But he is not God's equal, nor is he the primary enslaver of humanity.

His power is derivative, his influence is parasitic, and he thrives in ambiguity, operates through lies, and exploits whatever cracks Sin and Death have already carved into the human condition. He is a diplomat of disorder more than a king of darkness.

# BIBLIOGRAPHY

Abusch, T. (2015). The Witchcraft Series: Maqlū. Society of Biblial Literature Press.

Anderson, G. A. (2009). Sin: A History. Yale University Press.

Asma, S. T. (2009). On Monsters: An Unnatural History of Our Worst Fears. Oxford University Press.

Assmann, J. (2005). Death and Salvation in Ancient Egypt. Cornell University Press.

Assmann, J., and G. G. Stroumsa (eds.) (1999). Transformations of the Inner Self in Ancient Religions. Brill.

Baer, Y. (1936). Galut. Hebrew University Press.

Baker, R. (2022). Mesopotamian Civilization and the Origins of the New Testament. Cambridge University Press.

Barclay, J. M. G. (2015). Paul and the Gift. Eerdmans.

Barrett, C. K. (1991). The Epistle to the Romans (2nd ed.). A & C Black.

Bauckham, R. (2008). Jesus and the God of Israel: God Crucified and Other Studies on the New Testament's Christology of Divine Identity. Eerdmans.

Bauckham, R., and T. Hart (eds.). (1999). The Fate of the Dead: Studies on Jewish and Christian Apocalypses. Brill.

Beal, T. (2011). The Rise and Fall of the Bible. Houghton Mifflin.

Beal, T. (2022). Religion and Its Monsters (2nd ed.). Routledge.

Beker, J. C. (1980). Paul the Apostle: The Triumph of God in Life and Thought. Fortress Press.

Boccaccini, G. (2002). Roots of Rabbinic Judaism: An Intellectual History from Ezekiel to Daniel. Eerdmans.

Boyd, G. A. (1997). God at War: The Bible and Spiritual Conflict. IVP Academic.

Bruce, F. F. (1977). Paul: Apostle of the Heart Set Free. Eerdmans.

Bultmann, R. (1952). Theology of the New Testament. Scribner.

Byrne, B. (1996). Romans (SP 6). Liturgical Press.

Campbell, D. A. (2009). The Deliverance of God: An Apocalyptic Rereading of Justification in Paul. Eerdmans.

Charlesworth, J. H. (ed.). (1983–1985). The Old Testament Pseudepigrapha (2 vols.). Doubleday.

Chesnutt, R. D. (1995). From Death to Life: Conversion in Joseph and Aseneth. T & T Clark.

Cohen, J. J. (ed.). (1996). Monster Theory: Reading Culture. University of Minnesota Press.

Collins, J. J. (1998). The Apocalyptic Imagination: An Introduction to Jewish Apocalyptic Literature (2nd ed.). Eerdmans.

Cranfield, C. E. B. (1975). A Critical and Exegetical Commentary on the Epistle to the Romans I–VIII (ICC). T & T Clark.

Cranfield, C. E. B. (1979). A Critical and Exegetical Commentary on the Epistle to the Romans IX–XVI (ICC). T & T Clark.

Dalley, S. (2000). Myths from Mesopotamia: Creation, the Flood, Gilgamesh (rev. ed.). Oxford University Press.

Davies, D. J. (2002a). Anthropology and Theology. Berg.

Davies, D. J. (2002b). Death, Ritual and Belief. Continuum.

Davies, D. J. (2011). Emotion, Identity, and Religion. Oxford University Press.

Davies, J. (2022). "The Justice and Deliverance of God: Integrating Forensic and Cosmological in the 'Apocalyptic Paul.'" Currents in Biblical Research, 21(1), 78–88.

Day, J. (1985). God's Conflict with the Dragon and the Sea: Echoes of a Canaanite Myth in the Old Testament. Cambridge University Press.

Day, J. (2000). Yahweh and the Gods and Goddesses of Canaan. Sheffield Academic Press.

Deane, T. (2020). Monstrous Scripture: Race and the Bible in Modern Horror. Bloomsbury Academic.

de Boer, M. C. (2011). Galatians: A Commentary (NTL). Westminster John Knox.

Douglas, M. (1966). Purity and Danger. Routledge & Kegan Paul.

Dunn, J. D. G. (1970). Baptism in the Holy Spirit. SCM Press.

Dunn, J. D. G. (1975). "Romans 7:14–25 in the Theology of Paul." New Testament Studies, 21, 526–536.

Dunn, J. D. G. (1988). Romans 1–8 (WBC 38A). Word Books.

Dunn, J. D. G. (1988). Romans 9–16 (WBC 38B). Word Books.

Dunn, J. D. G. (1998). The Theology of Paul the Apostle. Eerdmans.

Eastman, S. G. (2007). Recovering Paul's Mother Tongue: Language and Theology in Galatians. Eerdmans.

Fee, G. D. (1994). God's Empowering Presence: The Holy Spirit in the Letters of Paul. Hendrickson.

Fewster, G. P. (2013). Creation Language in Romans 8. Brill.

Fitzmyer, J. A. (1993). Romans (AB 33). Doubleday.

Fletcher-Louis, C. H. T. (1997). Luke–Acts: Angels, Christology and Soteriology. Brill.

Fletcher-Louis, C. H. T. (2002). All the Glory of Adam: Liturgical Anthropology in the Dead Sea Scrolls. Brill.

Flusser, D. (1979). "Paul's Jewish Background." Proceedings of the Israel Academy of Sciences and Humanities, 7, 1–27.

Flusser, D. (1988). Judaism and the Origins of Christianity. Magnes Press.

Forger, D. L. (2018). "Divine Embodiment in Philo of Alexandria." Journal for the Study of Judaism, 49, 223–262.

Forger, D. L. (2020). "Jesus as God's Word(s): Aurality, Epistemology and Embodiment in the Gospel of John." Journal for the Study of the New Testament, 42, 274–302.

Forger, D. L. (2020). "God Made Manifest: Josephus, Idolatry, and Divine Images in Flavian Rome." Journal for the Study of Judaism, 51, 231–260.

Foster, B. R. (2005). Before the Muses: An Anthology of Akkadian Literature (3rd ed.). CDL Press.

Foucault, M. (1978). History of Sexuality, vol. 1. Hurley, R. (transl.). Pantheon Books.

Foucault, M. (1979). Discipline and Punish. Sheridan, A. (transl.). Vintage Books.

Foucault, M. (1980). Herculine Barbin. McDougall, R. (transl.). Pantheon Books.

Foucault, M. (1985). History of Sexuality, vol. 2. Hurley, R. (transl.). Pantheon Books.

Foucault, M. (1986). History of Sexuality, vol. 3. Hurley, R. (transl.). Pantheon Books.

Foucault, M. (1988). "Technologies of the Self." In Martin, L. H., H. Gutman, and P. H. Hutton (eds.). Technologies of the Self. Tavistock Publications, 16–49.

Foucault, M. (1998 [1967]). "Different Spaces." In Faubion, J. D. (ed.). Aesthetics, vol. 2. Hurley, R. (transl.). Allen Lane, 175–85.

Gaventa, B. R. (2004). "The Cosmic Power of Sin in Paul's Letter to the Romans: Toward a Widescreen Edition." Interpretation, 58, 229–240.

Gaventa, B. R. (2011). "Neither Height Nor Depth: Discerning the Cosmology of Romans." Scottish Journal of Theology, 64, 265–278.

Gaventa, B. R. (2016). When in Romans: An Invitation to Linger with the Gospel according to Paul. Baker Academic.

Gaventa, B. R. (2024). Romans: A Commentary (NTL). Westminster John Knox Press.

George, A. R. (2003). The Babylonian Gilgamesh Epic (2 vols.). Oxford University Press.

Gilmore, D. D. (2003). Monsters: Evil Beings, Mythical Beasts, and All Manner of Imaginary Terrors. University of Pennsylvania Press.

Gombis, T. G. (2009). The Drama of Ephesians: Participating in the Triumph of God. IVP Academic.

Gorman, M. J. (2009). Inhabiting the Cruciform God. Eerdmans.

Grafius, B. R. (2018). Reading the Bible with Horror. Lexington Books.

Hallo, W. W., and K. L. Younger (eds.). (1997–2002). The Context of Scripture (3 vols.). Brill.

Hamori, E. J. (2023). God's Monsters: Vengeful Spirits, Deadly Angels, Hybrid Creatures, and Divine Hitmen of the Bible. Broadleaf Books.

Harvey, J. D. (2019). A Commentary on Romans. Eisenbrauns.

Hays, R. B. (1989). Echoes of Scripture in the Letters of Paul. Yale University Press.

Hayward, C. T. R. (1996). The Jewish Temple: A Non-Biblical Sourcebook. Routledge.

Hayward, C. T. R. (2005). Interpretations of the Name Israel in Ancient Judaism and Some Early Christian Writings. Oxford University Press.

Hayward, C. T. R. (2010). Targums and the Transmission of Scripture into Judaism and Christianity. Brill.

Hengel, M. (1991). The Pre-Christian Paul. SCM Press.

Himmelfarb, M. (1993). Ascent to Heaven in Jewish and Christian Apocalypses. Oxford University Press.

Hoffner, H. A. (1998). Hittite Myths (2nd ed.). Society of Biblical Literature Press.

Hooker, M. D. (1990). From Adam to Christ: Essays on Paul. Cambridge University Press.

Horn, F. W. (1992). "Holy Spirit." In Freedman, D.N. (ed.). Anchor Bible Dictionary, vol. 3. Doubleday, 260–80.

Horn, F. W. (1992). Das Angeld des Geistes. Vandenhoeck & Ruprecht.

Horn, F. W. (1996). "Der Verzicht auf die Beschneidung im frühen Christentum." New Testament Studies 42, 479–505.

Hurtado, L. W. (2003). Lord Jesus Christ: Devotion to Jesus in Earliest Christianity. Eerdmans.

Jewett, R. (2007). Romans (Hermeneia). Fortress Press.

Kaplan, J. (2020). Monstrous Bodies: Biblical Imaginations of Disability. Oxford University Press.

Käsemann, E. (1933). Leib und Leib Christi. Mohr Siebeck.

Käsemann, E. (1937). "Das Abendmahl im Neuen Testament." In Asmussen, H. et al. (eds.). Abendmahlsgemeinschaft? Kaiser, 60–93.

Käsemann, E. (1964). Essays on New Testament Themes. SCM Press.

Käsemann, E. (1969). "Zur paulinischen Anthropologie." In Paulinische Perspektiven. Mohr Siebeck, 9–60.

Käsemann, E. (1971). Perspectives on Paul. Kohl, M. (transl.). SCM Press.

Käsemann, E. (1994). Commentary on Romans. Bromiley, G.W. (transl.). Eerdmans.

Keck, L. E. (2005). Romans (ANTC). Abingdon Press.

Klawans, J. (2006). Purity, Sacrifice, and the Temple. Oxford University Press.

Kotsko, A. (2016). The Prince of This World. Stanford University Press.

Kruse, C. G. (2012). Paul's Letter to the Romans (PNTC). Eerdmans.

Lakey, M. J. (2010). Image and Glory of God. T & T Clark.

Lakey, M. J. (2018). The Ritual World of Paul the Apostle. T & T Clark.

Lambert, W. G. (2013). Babylonian Creation Myths. Eisenbrauns.

Levenson, J. D. (1988). Creation and the Persistence of Evil. Princeton University Press.

Levenson, J. D. (2006). Resurrection and the Restoration of Israel. Yale University Press.

Levina, M., and D-M. T. Bui (2013). Monster Culture in the 21st Century: A Reader. Routledge.

Linebaugh, J. A. (2022). God, Grace, and Righteousness in Wisdom of Solomon and Paul's Letter to the Romans. Eerdmans.

Longarino, J. (2021). The Weight of Mortality: Paul's Apocalyptic Theology of Death. Ph.D. diss., Duke University.

Longenecker, R. N. (1990). Galatians (WBC, vol. 41). Word Books.

Longenecker, R. N. (2016). The Epistle to the Romans (NIGTC). Eerdmans.

Marzouk, S. H. (2015). Egypt as a Monster in the Book of Ezekiel. Eisenbrauns.

Martyn, J. L. (1997). Galatians: A New Translation with Introduction and Commentary (AB 33A). Doubleday.

Martin, D. B. (2014). The Corinthian Body (2nd ed.). Yale University Press.

Middleton, J. R. (2014). A New Heaven and a New Earth: Reclaiming Biblical Eschatology. Baker Academic.

Milgrom, J. (1991). Leviticus 1–16 (AB 3). Doubleday.

Milgrom, J. (1992). "The Priestly Concept of Holiness." In Miller, P. D., et al. (eds.). Ancient Israelite Religion. Fortress Press, 65–78.

Milgrom, J. (2000). Leviticus 17–22 (AB 3A). Doubleday.

Milgrom, J. (2001). Leviticus 23–27 (AB 3B). Doubleday.

Mittman, A. S. (2006). Maps and Monsters in Medieval England. Routledge.

Moo, D. J. (1996). The Epistle to the Romans (NICNT). Eerdmans.

Moo, D. J. (2018). The Letter to the Romans (rev. ed., NICNT). Eerdmans.

Morris, L. (1988). The Epistle to the Romans (PNTC). Eerdmans.

Murphy-O'Connor, J. (1993). "Paul in Arabia." Catholic Biblical Quarterly, 55, 732–737.

Murray, J. (1965). The Epistle to the Romans (NICNT). Eerdmans.

Nickelsburg, G. W. E. (2006). Jewish Literature between the Bible and the Mishnah (2nd ed.). Fortress Press.

Nygren, A. (1949). Commentary on Romans. Augsburg.

Osborne, G. R. (2004). Romans (IVPNTC). IVP Academic.

Pagels, E. (1988). Adam, Eve, and the Serpent. Vintage.

Pagels, E. (1995). The Origin of Satan. Vintage.

Pardee, D. (2002). Ritual and Cult at Ugarit. Society of Biblical Literature Press.

Putthoff, T. L. (2014). "Aseneth's Gastronomical Vision: Mystico-Theophagy and the New Creation in Joseph and Aseneth." Journal for the Study of the Pseudepigrapha 24, 96–117.

Putthoff, T. L. (2017). Ontological Aspects of Early Jewish Anthropology. Brill.

Putthoff, T. L. (2020). Gods and Humans in the Ancient Near East. Cambridge University Press.

Putthoff, T. L. (2021). "Anthropology." In Encyclopedia of Jewish-Christian Relations. Ehrensperger, K., et al. (eds.). Walter de Gruyter.

Putthoff, T. L. (2021a). "Mystery: Hebrew Bible." In Encyclopedia of the Bible and its Reception, vol. 19. Helmer, C., et al. (eds.). Walter de Gruyter.

Putthoff, T. L. (2021b). "Mystery: Judaism, Second Temple and Hellenistic Judaism." In Encyclopedia of the Bible and its Reception, vol. 19. Helmer, C., et al. (eds.). Walter de Gruyter.

Putthoff, T. L. (2021c). "Mystery: New Testament." In Encyclopedia of the Bible and its Reception, vol. 19. Helmer, C., et al. (eds.). Walter de Gruyter.

Putthoff, T. (2025a). Jesus: The StrategicO Life and Mission of the Messiah and His Movement, vol. 1—A Handbook. Hekhal Publishing Co.

Putthoff, T. (2025b). Jesus: The Strategic Life and Mission of the Messiah and His Movement, vol. 2—The Story. Hekhal Publishing Co.

Putthoff, T. (2025c). Jesus: The Strategic Life and Mission of the Messiah and His Movement, vol. 3—Behind the Story. Hekhal Publishing Co.

Rabens, V. (2013). The Holy Spirit and Ethics in Paul (2nd rev. ed.). Mohr Siebeck.

Rabens, V. (2014a). "Ethics and the Spirit in Paul (1)." Expository Times 125, 209–19.

Rabens, V. (2014b). "Ethics and the Spirit in Paul (2)." Expository Times 125, 272–81.

Rabens, V. (2014c). "Pneuma and the Beholding of God." In Frey, J., and J. R. Levison (eds.). The Holy Spirit, Inspiration, and the Cultures of Antiquity. Walter de Gruyter, 293–330.

Rabens, V. (2016). "The Holy Spirit and Deification in Paul." In Dragutinovic, P., K.-W. Niebuhr, J. B. Wallace, and C. Karakolis (eds.). The Holy Spirit and the Church according to the New Testament. Mohr Siebeck, 187–220.

Rehfeld, E.L. (2012). Relationale Ontologie bei Paulus. Mohr Siebeck.

Safrai, S. (1974). "Jewish Self-Understanding in the First Century." In Safrai, S., and M. Stern (eds.). The Jewish People in the First Century, vol. 1. Brill, 457–496.

Safrai, S. (1985). The Jewish People in the First Century (Heb. ed.). Magnes Press.

Sanders, E. P. (1977). Paul and Palestinian Judaism. Fortress Press.

Schnelle, U. (2009). Theology of the New Testament. Baker Academic.

Schreiner, T. R. (1998). Romans (BECNT). Baker Academic.

Schreiner, T. R. (2018). Romans (2nd ed., BECNT). Baker Academic.

Scurlock, J. (1995). "Death and the Afterlife in Ancient Mesopotamian Thought." In Sasson, J.M., and J. Baines (eds.). Civilizations of the Ancient Near East, vol. 3. Charles Scribner's Sons, 1883–1893.

Segal, A. F. (1990). Paul the Convert. Yale University Press.

Segal, A. F. (1994). Life After Death. Doubleday.

Schweitzer, A. (1912). Paul and His Interpreters. Montgomery, W. (transl.). A & C Black.

Schweitzer, A. (1931). The Mysticism of Paul the Apostle. Montgomery, W. (transl.). Crossroad.

Simons, F. (2017). Burn your Way to Success: Studies in the Mesopotamian Ritual and Incantation Series Šurpu. PhD thesis, University of Birmingham.

Skal, D. J. (1993). The Monster Show: A Cultural History of Horror. Norton & Co.

Smith, M. S. (1994). The Ugaritic Baal Cycle, vol. I. Brill.

Smith, M. S. (2001). The Origins of Biblical Monotheism: Israel's Polytheistic Background and the Ugaritic Texts. Oxford University Press.

Snell, D. C. (1997). Life in the Ancient Near East, 3100–332 BCE. Yale University Press.

Snell, D. C. (2001). A Companion to the Ancient Near East. Blackwell.

Snell, D. C. (2011). Ancient Near East: The Basics. Routledge.

Snell, D. C. (2014). The Etymological Origins of Ancient Near Eastern Concepts of the Self. In Stackert, J., B. Niditch, and C. Levin (eds.). The Idea of Biblical Interpretation: Essays in Honor of James L. Kugel. Brill, 117–134.

Snell, D. C. (2017). A Guide to Reading the Ancient Near East. Blackwell.

Stowers, S. K. (1994). A Rereading of Romans: Justice, Jews, and Gentiles. Yale University Press.

Stuckenbruck, L. T. (2014). The Myth of Rebellious Angels: Studies in Second Temple Judaism and New Testament Texts. Mohr Siebeck.

Stuckenbruck, L. T., and G. Boccaccini (eds.). (2016). Enoch and the Synoptic Gospels. Eerdmans.

Talbert, C. H. (2002). Romans. Smyth & Helwys.

Taylor, J. H. (2001). Death and the Afterlife in Ancient Egypt. The University of Chicago Press.

Terrien, S. (1978). The Elusive Presence. Harper & Row.

Tilling, C. (2012). Paul's Divine Christology. Mohr Siebeck.

Turner, V. (1969). The Ritual Process: Structure and Anti-Structure. Aldine.

Twelftree, G. H. (1993). Jesus the Exorcist: A Contribution to the Study of the Historical Jesus. Mohr Siebeck.

van Gennep, A. (1909). Les Rites de Passage. Emile Nourry.

van Kooten, G. H. (2003). Cosmic Christology in Paul and the Pauline School. Mohr Siebeck.

van Kooten, G. H. (2008). Paul's Anthropology in Context. Mohr Siebeck.

Wallace, J. B. (2011). Snatched Into Paradise (2 Cor 12:1–10). Walter de Gruyter.

Waltke, B. K., and M. P. O'Connor (1990). An Introduction to Biblical Hebrew Syntax. Eisenbrauns.

Walton, J. H. (1989). Ancient Israelite Literature in Its Cultural Context. Zondervan.

Walton, J. H. (2009). The Lost World of Genesis One. InterVarsity Press.

Walton, J. H. (2011). Genesis 1 as Ancient Cosmology. Eisenbrauns.

Wasserman, E. (2008). The Death of the Soul in Romans 7: Sin, Death, and the Law in Light of Hellenistic Moral Psychology. Mohr Siebeck.

Williams, R. (2016). The Edge of Words: God and the Habits of Language. Bloomsbury.

Wilson, B. E. (2021). The Embodied God: Seeing the Divine in Luke-Acts and the Early Church. Oxford University Press.

Wilson, B. E. (2024). "God's Body and the Material Turn: Divine (Im)Materiality in Biblical Theophanies." Harvard Theological Review, 117, 607–630.

Witherington III, B. (1995). Conflict at Corinth. Eerdmans.

Witherington III, B. (2004). Paul's Letter to the Romans. Eerdmans.

Witherington III, B. (2011). Paul's Letter to the Philippians. Eerdmans.

Wright, D. P. (1987). The Disposal of Impurity: Elimination Rites in the Bible and in Hittite and Mesopotamian Literature. Scholars Press.

Wright, N. T. (1992). The New Testament and the People of God. Fortress Press.

Wright, N. T. (2002). Romans (NIB, vol. 10). Abingdon Press.

Wright, N. T. (2013). Paul and the Faithfulness of God. Fortress Press.

Wright, N. T. (2018). Paul: A Biography. HarperOne.

Wyatt, N. (1998). Religious Texts from Ugarit. Sheffield Academic Press.

Ziesler, J. A. (1989). Paul's Letter to the Romans (TNTC). IVP Academic.

# INDEXES

13:11, 7
17, 133
18, 133

18:11–13, 133
20:14, 7, 51, 147

## Index of Subjects

www.ingramcontent.com/pod-product-compliance
Lightning Source LLC
Chambersburg PA
CBHW051624120626

46551CB00014B/1919